my **revision** notes

OCR AS/A-level History

THE FRENCH REVOLUTION AND THE RULE OF NAPOLEON

1774–1815

Mike Wells
Dave Martin

Series editor
Nicholas Fellows

HODDER EDUCATION
AN HACHETTE UK COMPANY

Orders: please contact Bookpoint Ltd, 130 Milton Park, Abingdon, Oxon OX14 4SE. Telephone: +44 (0)1235 827720. Fax: +44 (0)1235 400454. Email education@bookpoint.co.uk Lines are open from 9 a.m. to 5 p.m., Monday to Saturday, with a 24-hour message answering service. You can also order through our website: www.hoddereducation.co.uk

ISBN: 978 1 4718 7603 5

First published in 2017 by

Hodder Education,

An Hachette UK Company

Carmelite House

50 Victoria Embankment

London EC4Y 0DZ

www.hoddereducation.co.uk

Impression number 10 9 8 7 6 5 4 3 2 1

Year 2021 2020 2019 2018 2017

Illustrations by Integra
Typeset by Integra
Printed in Spain

A catalogue record for this title is available from the British Library.

My Revision Planner

Introduction

Unit 2: Non-British Period Study

Component 2 involves the study of a period of non-British history and at AS level will also involve the evaluation of a historical interpretation from one of two named topics. The types of essay set for both AS and A-level are similar, but the AS mark scheme does not have a Level 6 (see page 7).

The French Revolution and the rule of Napoleon, 1774–1815

The specification lists the content under four key topics:

Key topic 1 – The causes of the French Revolution from 1774 and the events of 1789

Key topic 2 – The Revolution from October 1789 to the Directory, 1795

Key topic 3 – Napoleon Bonaparte to 1807

Key topic 4 – The decline and fall of Napoleon, 1807–15

Although each period of study is set out in chronological sections in the specification, an exam question may arise from one or more of these sections.

AS-level

The AS-level examination which you may be taking includes all the content on the specification.

You are required to answer:

- Section A: ONE question from a choice of TWO. They are traditional essays and will require you to use your knowledge to explain, analyse and assess key features of the period studied, and then reach a judgement about the issue in the question. The question is worth 30 marks.
- Section B: ONE interpretation question. The specification names the two key topics from which the interpretation will be drawn. Questions will require you to evaluate the strengths and limitations of a given historical interpretation, in the form of either one or two sentences, by applying your own knowledge and awareness of the debate to the given interpretation. The question is worth 20 marks.

The exam lasts one and a half hours, and you are advised to spend slightly more time on Section A.

At AS-level, Unit 2 will be worth a total of 50 marks and is worth 50 per cent of the AS-level examination.

A-Level

The A-level examination at the end of the course includes all the content on the specification.

You are required to answer ONE question with TWO parts from a choice of TWO questions:

- Each question will have TWO parts. Question (a) will be a short essay in which you are asked to analyse two issues and reach a judgement as to which is the more important or significant. Question (b) is a traditional period study essay and will require you to use your knowledge to explain, analyse and assess key features of the period studied and then reach a judgement about the issue in the question.
- The short essay is worth 10 marks and the traditional essay is worth 20 marks.
- The two parts of each question will be drawn from different parts of the specification.

The exam lasts for one hour. You should spend about 20 minutes on Question (a) and 40 minutes on Question (b).

At A-level Unit 2 will be worth a total of 30 marks and 15 per cent of the A-level examination.

In both the AS and A-level examinations you are being tested on the ability to:

- use relevant knowledge
- analyse factors and reach a judgement.

In the AS-level examination you are also being tested on your ability to analyse and evaluate the different ways in which aspects of the past have been interpreted.

How to use this book

This book has been designed to help you develop the knowledge and skills necessary to succeed in the examination.

The book is divided into four sections – one for each section of the AS and A-level specifications. Each section is made up of a series of topics organised into double-page spreads:

- On the left-hand page you will find a summary of the key content you will need to learn. Words in bold in the key content are defined in the glossary (see pages 86–88).
- On the right-hand page you will find exam-focused activities.

Together these two strands of the book will provide you with the knowledge and skills essential for examination success.

▼ Key historical content

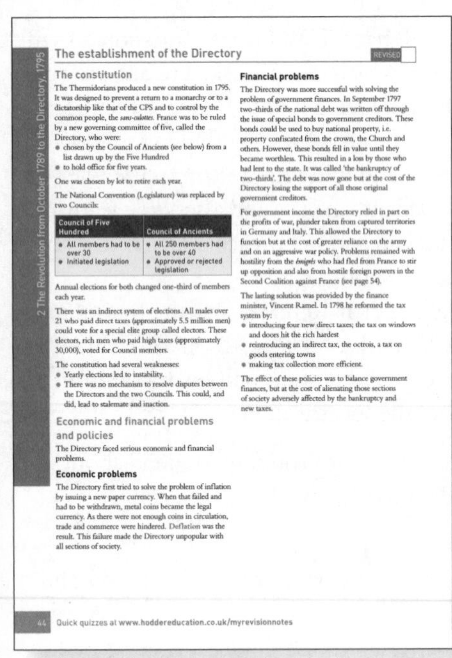

2 The Revolution from October 1789 to the Directory, 1795

The establishment of the Directory

REVISED

The constitution

The Thermidorians produced a new constitution in 1795. It was designed to prevent a return to a monarchy or to a dictatorship like that of the CPS and to control by the common people, the *sans-culottes*. France was to be ruled by a new governing committee of five, called the Directory, who were:

- chosen by the Council of Ancients (see below) from a list drawn up by the Five Hundred
- to hold office for five years.

One was chosen by lot to retire each year.

The National Convention (Legislature) was replaced by two Councils:

Council of Five Hundred	Council of Ancients
• All members had to be over 30 • Initiated legislation	• All 250 members had to be over 40 • Approved or rejected legislation

Annual elections for both changed one-third of members each year.

There was an indirect system of elections. All males over 21 who paid direct taxes (approximately 5.5 million men) could vote for a special elite group called electors. These electors, rich men who paid high taxes (approximately 30,000), voted for Council members.

The constitution had several weaknesses:

- Yearly elections led to instability.
- There was no mechanism to resolve disputes between the Directors and the two Councils. This could, and did, lead to stalemate and inaction.

Economic and financial problems and policies

The Directory faced serious economic and financial problems.

Economic problems

The Directory first tried to solve the problem of inflation by issuing a new paper currency. When that failed and had to be withdrawn, metal coins became the legal currency. As there were not enough coins in circulation, trade and commerce were hindered. Deflation was the result. This failure made the Directory unpopular with all sections of society.

Financial problems

The Directory was more successful with solving the problem of government finances. In September 1797 two-thirds of the national debt was written off through the issue of special bonds to government creditors. These bonds could be used to buy national property, i.e. property confiscated from the crown, the Church and others. However, these bonds fell in value until they became worthless. This resulted in a loss by those who had lent to the state. It was called 'the bankruptcy of two-thirds'. The debt was now gone but at the cost of the Directory losing the support of all those original government creditors.

For government income the Directory relied in part on the profits of war, plunder taken from captured territories in Germany and Italy. This allowed the Directory to function but at the cost of greater reliance on the army and on an aggressive war policy. Problems remained with hostility from the *émigrés* who had fled from France to stir up opposition and also from hostile foreign powers in the Second Coalition against France (see page 54).

The lasting solution was provided by the finance minister, Vincent Ramel. In 1798 he reformed the tax system by:

- introducing four new direct taxes; the tax on windows and doors hit the rich hardest
- reintroducing an indirect tax, the octrois, a tax on goods entering towns
- making tax collection more efficient.

The effect of these policies was to balance government finances, but at the cost of alienating those sections of society adversely affected by the bankruptcy and new taxes.

44 Quick quizzes at www.hoddereducation.co.uk/myrevisionnotes

▼ Exam-focused activities

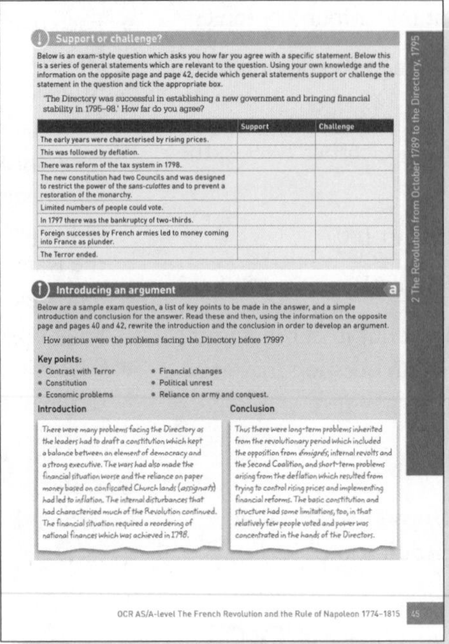

Support or challenge?

Below is an exam-style question which asks you how far you agree with a specific statement. Below this is a series of general statements which are relevant to the question. Using your own knowledge and the information on the opposite page and page 42, decide which general statements support or challenge the statement in the question and tick the appropriate box.

'The Directory was successful in establishing a new government and bringing financial stability in 1795–98.' How far do you agree?

	Support	Challenge
The early years were characterised by rising prices.		
This was followed by deflation.		
There was reform of the tax system in 1798.		
The new constitution had two Councils and was designed to restrict the power of the *sans-culottes* and to prevent a restoration of the monarchy.		
Limited numbers of people could vote.		
In 1797 there was the bankruptcy of two-thirds.		
Foreign successes by French armies led to money coming into France as plunder.		
The Terror ended.		

Introducing an argument

a

Below are a sample exam question, a list of key points to be made in the answer, and a simple introduction and conclusion for the answer. Read these and then, using the information on the opposite page and pages 40 and 42, rewrite the introduction and the conclusion in order to develop an argument.

How serious were the problems facing the Directory before 1799?

Key points:

- Contrast with Terror
- Constitution
- Economic problems
- Financial changes
- Political unrest
- Reliance on army and conquest.

Introduction

There were many problems facing the Directory as the leaders had to draft a constitution which kept a balance between an element of democracy and a strong executive. The wars had also made the financial situation worse and the reliance on paper money based on confiscated Church lands (*assignats*) had led to inflation. The internal disturbances that had characterised much of the Revolution continued. The financial situation required a reordering of national finances which was achieved in 1798.

Conclusion

Thus there were long-term problems inherited from the revolutionary period which included the opposition from *émigrés*, internal revolts and the Second Coalition, and short-term problems arising from the deflation which resulted from trying to control rising prices and implementing financial reforms. The basic constitution and structure had some limitations, too, in that relatively few people voted and power was concentrated in the hands of the Directors.

2 The Revolution from October 1789 to the Directory, 1795

OCR AS/A-level The French Revolution and the Rule of Napoleon 1774–1815 45

Examination activities

There are three levels of exam-focused activities:

- **Band 1** activities are designed to develop the foundation skills needed to pass the exam. These have a green heading and this symbol:
- **Band 2** activities are designed to build on the skills developed in Band 1 activities and to help you to achieve a C grade. These have an orange heading and this symbol:
- **Band 3** activities are designed to enable you to access the highest grades. These have a purple heading and this symbol:

Some of the activities have answers or suggested answers on pages 93–96. These have the following symbol to indicate this:

Each section ends with exam-style questions and sample answers with commentary. This will give you guidance on what is expected to achieve the top grade.

You can also keep track of your revision by ticking off each topic heading in the book, or by ticking the checklist on the contents page. Tick each box when you have:

- revised and understood a topic
- completed the activities.

Mark schemes

For some of the activities in the book it will be useful to refer to the mark schemes for this paper. Below are abbreviated forms.

AS-level

Level	Essay	Interpretation
5	Mostly focused, supported answer with good analysis and evaluation to reach a supported judgement. **25–30**	Very good analysis of the interpretation, aware of the debate and uses detailed knowledge to evaluate the strengths and limitations. **17–20**
4	Some focus with support, analysis with limited evaluation and judgement. **19–24**	Good analysis of the interpretation, some awareness of the debate and uses knowledge to evaluate the strengths and limitations. **13–16**
3	Partial focus on the question, with some knowledge and analysis, but little or no judgement. **13–18**	Partial analysis of the interpretation, some knowledge and awareness of the debate. May be limited in treatment of strength or limitations. **9–12**
2	Focus is descriptive and may be more on the topic than the question. Any analysis may be implied. **7–12**	Limited analysis, may describe the interpretation and the debate. Any evaluation is implied or superficial. **5–8**
1	Focus is on the topic and attempts at analysis will be little more than assertion. **1–6**	Focused more on the topic than the given interpretation. Knowledge is general and evaluation is asserted. **1–4**

A-level

Level	Short answer essay	Essay
6	Analyses and evaluates both factors with detailed knowledge to reach a developed judgement. **9–10**	Well-focused, supported answer with very good analysis and developed evaluation to reach a supported and sustained judgement. **17–20**
5	Analyses and evaluates both factors with some knowledge to reach a developed judgement. **7–8**	Mostly focused, supported answer with good analysis and evaluation to reach a supported judgement. **13–16**
4	Some analysis and evaluation of both factors, with some support and judgement. **5–6**	Some focus with support, analysis with limited evaluation and judgement. **10–12**
3	Partial analysis and evaluation with some knowledge to reach a basic judgement. **3–4**	Partial focus on the question, with some knowledge and analysis, but little or no judgement. **7–9**
2	Limited analysis and knowledge, with a simple judgement. **2**	Focus is descriptive and may be more on the topic than the question. Any analysis may be implied. **4–6**
1	General analysis and knowledge with assertion. **1**	Focus on the topic and attempts at analysis will be little more than assertion. **1–3**

1 The causes of the French Revolution from 1774 and the events of 1789

The structure of the Ancien Régime

REVISED

Social divisions

In the eighteenth century, France was divided into 'estates', or social classes. These were official divisions, and affected legal status and taxation.

The First Estate – the clergy

The clergy formed less than 0.5 per cent of the population but the Church owned roughly one-tenth of French land. It controlled almost all education, most hospitals and **poor relief**. It had powers of censorship and published the government's messages. In many towns the clergy dominated while in the countryside the parish priest (*curé*) was influential.

The Second Estate – the nobility

There were roughly 120,000 nobles, less than one per cent of the population, but they owned between a quarter and a third of French land. There were three levels within the nobility:

- The *noblesse d'epée* lived with the King in the palace at Versailles and were very wealthy, provided the King's advisers, ambassadors, **intendants** and ministers and had access to **royal patronage**.
- The *noblesse de robe* were nobles created by the monarchy selling legal and administrative offices in return for a hereditary title. In 1789 there were over 70,000 **venal offices**.
- Most other nobles lived on their country estates. Many were not wealthy. They were jealous of court nobles, protective of their own status and privileges, and dependent on their **feudal rights**.

The Third Estate

The Third Estate made up the rest of society and consisted of nearly 28 million people:

- At the top were the **bourgeoisie** (middle class), who lived mostly in towns. By 1789 they were growing in wealth and numbers. They owned most industrial and all commercial capital, about one-fifth of all private French wealth and roughly one-quarter of French land. Often their ambition was to become part of the nobility.
- In the countryside were the peasants, over 80 per cent of the population. The majority farmed at **subsistence** level and worked as labourers on the land, in industries or as migrant workers in towns.
- In the towns were the small property owners, skilled workers and unskilled labourers.

Privileges and burdens

The First and Second Estates had considerable privileges. The clergy paid no taxes. Instead the Church made a voluntary annual grant of about 16 million **livres**, just 5 per cent of total Church income. The nobility were exempt from the heaviest tax, the *taille* (land tax), and the *corvées royales* (labour service on the roads). They paid some newer taxes linked to income but were often able to avoid paying the full amount. They were exempt from military **conscription** although many volunteered to fight by buying **commissions**. The bourgeoisie, though often richer than the nobles, were frustrated because the nobles dominated the higher posts in the army and the Church and had tax privileges denied to commoners. Thus a well-educated and prosperous part of French society was increasingly resentful.

The peasantry which included some of the poorest in society, carried the heaviest burden. To the lord of the manor (the *seigneur*) they paid rents and taxes on their grain harvest and some had to do labour service. To the state they paid the *taille* and the *gabelle* (salt tax). They also did labour service on the roads. They could be conscripted or have soldiers **billeted** upon them. They paid the **tithe** to the Church. For many, their main concern was to stay alive and this was dependent on the price of bread. Many richer peasants resented the burden of dues and taxes.

Mind map

Make a copy of the mind map below and use the information on the opposite page and page 10 to add detail to it, showing how French society was divided before 1789.

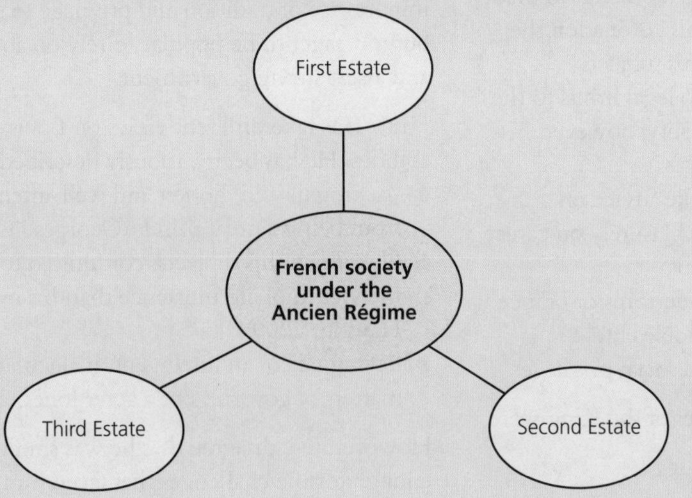

Turning assertion into argument

a

Below are a sample question and a series of assertions. Read the exam question and then add a justification to each of the assertions to turn each one into an argument.

'The Ancien Régime was a deeply unjust society.' How far do you agree?

The first two estates had too much privilege because ...

____

____

The peasantry was particularly harmed because ...

____

____

Middle-class grievances were important because ...

____

____

The qualities of Louis XVI as King of France

REVISED

Absolutism

The head of the Ancien Régime was the King. In theory he was an '**absolute monarch**'. At his coronation the King swore an oath to God, not to his subjects. Absolutism means that there were no legal limits to the King's power over his subjects. In reality, however, his power was limited:

- **Louis XVI** had been taught to take advice on important decisions and it was usual to rely on career administrators and courtiers for this.
- Louis was bound by the laws and customs of France.
- Louis needed the consent of the noble elite.
- There were deep-rooted local and social privileges.

However, the personality and abilities of the King were still important.

Louis XVI (ruled 1774–92, executed 1793)

Louis Auguste de France, Duc de Berri, was the third child of Louis, son of King Louis XV. His parents took little interest in him and he did not become **dauphin** until he was eleven, following the death of both his elder brother and his father. He was not unintelligent and was adept in Italian and English, but was a withdrawn and shy boy. He was married at the age of fifteen to the fourteen-year-old Austrian princess Maria Antonia (**Marie Antoinette**). Their first child was not born until eight years later.

Though he relished the ceremonies of kingship he did not enjoy the luxuries that went with it or the grandeur of monarchy. He enjoyed hunting, poring over naval plans, ship design and lock making. He was, by nature, anxious and apprehensive, and was oppressed by a sense of duty. He did not command immediate respect as a person, and was awkward and ill-at-ease on social occasions. He was indecisive and uncommunicative, and had limited ability to analyse problems and situations. He consistently failed to act decisively to solve the problems about which he worried so much.

Louis was kind, with a rough sense of humour. He believed in the divine nature of his kingship; he was religiously devout and had a strong sense of mission to protect the Church. In many ways he was a modern monarch and took an interest in improvements for his people and all affairs of state. However, he lacked the decisive character needed to steer France through the problems it faced. He was too conscious of the importance of tradition and privilege to sweep it away, but too eager to be popular to rely on absolute authority and assert strong government.

Historians take different views on Louis' character and abilities. He has been variously described as:

- 'lacking in will; honest and well-intentioned ... far from being a great mind' (Georges Lefebvre, 1939)
- 'devoted to his subjects, committed to reform, more the victim of circumstance than his own failings' (Paul Hanson, 2009)
- having taken 'an intelligent, if fluctuating interest in matters of government' (Peter Jones, 2010).

However, few disagree that he was simply not strong enough for the challenges that faced him.

Problems of government

Government, based in the Palace of Versailles, consisted of Louis, his advisers and ministers. Louis decided the overall direction of government policy and met his ministers individually to discuss the work of their department, rather than making decisions collectively. This created the problem of ministers and **court factions** working against each other, not co-operating. Dealing with these issues was hard for a King who lacked good communication skills and a decisive personality.

A second problem was the wide variation in laws and customs. France had no single representative body covering the whole country. All royal legislation had to be **ratified** by one of the thirteen regional **parlements**. France was a patchwork of different forms of administration, different legal systems, different taxes and different rules on who paid them. So there was no single solution to any problem. Previous kings had attempted to create one system by splitting the country into 36 ***généralités***, or administrative areas, each under the control of a royal official, an intendant. The intendants were hindered by local law courts and parlements and seen as overly authoritarian. What was needed was decisive modernisation and reform, but this could only come from strong leadership from the King or consistent support of able reforming ministers. Again, Louis was not able to deliver.

Delete as applicable

Below are a sample exam question and a paragraph written in answer to this question. Read the paragraph and decide which of the possible options (in bold) is the most appropriate.

'Louis XVI was an inadequate king.' How far do you agree?

It is **fair/unfair** to argue that Louis was in himself an inadequate king. The limits on his power in practice were **considerable/limited/minimal.** The system of government he inherited was **very effective/not very efficient/very disorganised** and weak. France itself was **divided/very united** and **under central control/easy to govern.** However, the royal intendants **could rule as they wished in the King's name/faced opposition/were very weak.** Louis' popularity was **helped/hindered/unaffected** by his marriage to Marie Antoinette. The King himself **took no interest in government/was very effective in bringing about reforms/took an interest in affairs of state.** An important part of his view of kingship was his **belief in/dislike of/determination to change** traditional privileges.

Support your judgement

Read the following sample exam question and two basic judgements. Support the judgement that you agree with most strongly by adding a reason that justifies the judgement.

Tip: Whichever option you choose you will have to weigh up both sides of the argument. You could use words such as 'whereas' or 'although' in order to help the process of evaluation.

'Before 1789, the French monarchy was absolute in theory but not in practice.'

The power of the King was more apparent than actual because ...

____

____

The monarchy was absolute because ...

____

____

Financial problems and attempts by Turgot, Necker and Calonne to deal with them

REVISED

Royal debt

In 1774 Louis XVI's biggest problem was money. The monarchy was heavily in debt due to the costs of foreign wars:

War	Estimated cost
War of Austrian Succession (1740–48)	1 billion livres
Seven Years' War (1756–63)	1.8 billion livres

Louis could not pay off the debt. Even in peacetime royal income was not enough to cover expenditure because of the size of the interest payments. In the short term the crown borrowed from international banks but in the long term this just made things worse. The decision to go to war in support of the **American colonies** against Britain made the financial situation worse.

Inefficient tax system

Most royal income came from taxation. This was not enough because:

- The nobles, the King's richest subjects, were exempt from most taxes.
- Tax collection was both chaotic and incomplete because of all the regional differences.
- **Tax farming** reduced the crown's income. The **Farmers-General** paid an agreed sum in advance for the right to collect certain taxes. What they collected above that sum was their profit.

Attempts to improve royal finances

Louis tried to follow a policy of reform to improve royal finances. The Controller General was the minister responsible.

Turgot

In 1774 Louis appointed Anne-Robert-Jacques Turgot as Controller General. Turgot was influenced by the ideas of the **physiocrats**. He removed price controls and abolished guilds and proposed a new property tax. His reforms and the way he went about them aroused great hostility from those whose interests were threatened. Louis dismissed him in 1776.

Necker

Instead, in 1777, Jacques **Necker**, a Swiss banker, was appointed. He tried a different route of reforming royal expenditure and increasing the royal share of farmed taxes. He tried to cut venal offices, but this drew hostility from the nobles who held them.

Necker's key mistake was advising Louis that France could afford to enter the American War of Independence when it could not. This war cost an estimated 1.3 billion livres, so royal debt increased.

In 1781 Necker issued the first public report on royal finances to show that, in his view, they were in good order. However, some of the minor details of court expenditure were seized upon as examples of extravagant royal spending by enemies of the monarchy. This lost Necker the support of the court and he resigned.

Calonne

From 1783 Louis' chief minister, the Vicomte de Calonne, managed the royal finances by selling offices and by lavish spending. The spending maintained confidence in the monarchy, which meant that it could raise loans. However, Calonne recognised that this could not continue indefinitely and that reform was still needed. He hoped to make changes when a number of taxes were due for renewal in 1787. But events overtook him. Calonne was unsuccessful in raising loans in 1785, and in early 1786 and in August 1786 he told Louis that the government was close to bankruptcy.

The financial situation by 1789 was particularly bad, with a deficit of 126 million livres and interest on debt taking 51 per cent of total spending – more than the 36 per cent spent on defence.

Importance of financial problems

The financial problems were of great importance because they revealed the weakness of the crown and opened the King and Queen to accusations of extravagance. They also led to attempts to involve the nation in reforms of finance, first by calling a special Assembly of Notables in 1787 (see page 18) and then the consultative and legislative assembly of the different classes of France that had met intermittently between 1302 and 1614, the **Estates General**, in 1789. It was this that led to the Revolution.

Introducing an argument

a

Below are a sample exam question, a list of key points to be made in the answer, and a simple introduction and conclusion for the answer. Read these and then, using the information on the opposite page, rewrite the introduction and the conclusion in order to develop an argument.

Assess the importance of financial problems for Louis XVI and his ministers before 1789.

Key points:

- Financial problems showed the weakness of the Ancient Régime.
- The crown had to raise more taxes to pay off interest payments.
- The privileged orders would not co-operate.
- Louis was forced to dismiss reforming ministers, which showed him to be weak.
- Financial problems forced Louis to agree to call the Estates General in 1789.

Introduction

There were many financial problems by 1789 which had been brought about by the debates caused by wars. Louis XVI added to the problems by entering the War of American Independence. The crown was near to bankruptcy and a number of leading ministers had tried and failed to bring about reforms. The financial problems showed everyone how selfish the nobles were in opposing new taxes and they also led to the calling of the Estates General in 1789, which began the chain of events leading to revolution.

Conclusion

To conclude, there were many reasons why finance was the most pressing problem for the French monarchy before 1789 and did most to bring about the Revolution. It is linked to the other main problem, the weakness of the King, and also to the great social problems of an unjust and privileged society.

Develop the detail

a

Below are a sample exam question and a paragraph written in answer to this question. The paragraph contains a limited amount of detail. Annotate the paragraph to add additional detail to the answer.

Assess the reasons why finance remained such a problem for Louis XVI before 1789.

The financial problems remained such a problem because different royal ministers with different views about the issue could not find a permanent solution and their reforms caused unrest and opposition which the King could not overcome. The determination of the privileged classes not to accept any change which would seem to undermine their privilege was another important factor. They portrayed financial reform as 'tyranny' and undermined attempts by ministers to make changes. Also, the continuing failure to get reform led Louis to agree to special assemblies to discuss the issue and get agreement. This was to prove a major problem because when other meetings failed, he agreed to call the Estates General.

The ideas of the Enlightenment and the impact of the American Revolution

REVISED

The Enlightenment

The intellectual movement known as the Enlightenment spread across Europe in the eighteenth century. Writers and thinkers challenged a wide range of views that were accepted at the time about religion, nature and absolute monarchy. They considered the nature of society and men's relationships with each other, exploring ideas of freedom, liberty and equality. The Enlightenment had a particularly strong influence in France.

Extent of influence in France – the *philosophes*

The Enlightenment's leading writers and thinkers in France were the *philosophes*. Many of them contributed to the most important work of the French Enlightenment – *The Encyclopaedia*, edited by Diderot and published 1750–72. Its aim was 'to change the way people think'. Articles dealt with topics like 'reason' but also with agricultural techniques, printing and metalworking. Its scientific approach directly challenged ideas held by the Church and other institutions, and caused huge controversy. Some in the Church wanted it suppressed.

The most influential *philosophes* were Montesquieu, Voltaire and **Rousseau**. They expressed a deep dislike of organised religion and discussed how social and political institutions might be changed for the good of the people. They questioned the institutions of the Ancien Régime but did not advocate revolution.

- Montesquieu criticised royal absolutism, but argued that it was the role of the aristocracy to limit royal power, not the people.
- Voltaire criticised the Catholic Church and religious intolerance, but believed religion was necessary to preserve public morals. He also defended royal authority.
- Rousseau went furthest. He argued that a **despotic** monarch could be overthrown by their subjects and that sovereignty resided in the people, rather than just in the person of the King.

The *philosophes*' ideas reached a wider audience through their stories and plays. Voltaire's popular novel, *Candide*, was banned for blasphemy, and Voltaire was imprisoned in the fortress in Paris known as the Bastille.

Salons

Enlightenment ideas were often spread through the **salons**. An aristocratic hostess would invite a range of guests, nobles and bourgeoisie, to discuss art, literature and politics. On occasion, political decisions were taken and deals made between the King's ministers in salons.

The new ideas were also discussed in the increasing number of cafes and **Masonic Lodges**, and in the growing numbers of newspapers: there were three newspapers in 1700 but over 80 by 1785.

The impact of the American Revolution and War of Independence

America was another source of ideas challenging the Ancien Régime. Louis XVI had taken the fateful decision to enter the War of Independence in 1778. The American colonies had been in revolt against British rule for two years and many in France were sympathetic to the colonists' cause of freedom (liberty) and democracy. Some idealistic French aristocrats, notably the **Marquis de Lafayette**, had already crossed the Atlantic to enlist in the American forces. When they and the 8,000 troops who served in America came home after 1783 they brought with them the renewed ideas of liberty and democracy, as well as the example and experience of the overthrow of an existing political authority and the building of a new order in its place.

Challenge the historian

a

Below is a sample AS exam question including an interpretation written by a historian. You must read the extract, identify the argument in the interpretation, and use your own knowledge to support and provide a counter-argument, challenging the interpretation offered.

'Had the Enlightenment put forward a real programme for political change? Probably not, but there is no denying that the Enlightenment encouraged probing criticism and led to calls for reform.'

Adapted from: Francis Ford, *Europe 1780–1830* (1970)

Evaluate the strengths and limitations of this interpretation, making reference to other interpretations that you have studied.

1 What is the view of the interpretation?

2 What knowledge of your own do you have that supports the interpretation?

3 What knowledge of your own do you have that challenges the interpretation?

Spectrum of importance

Below are a sample exam question and a list of general points which could be used to answer the question. Use your own knowledge and the information on the opposite page and pages 8, 10 and 12 to reach a judgement about the importance of these general points to the question posed. Write numbers on the spectrum below to indicate their relative importance. Having done this, write a brief justification of your placement, explaining why some of these factors are more important than others. The resulting diagram could form the basis of an essay plan.

How serious were the problems facing the Ancien Régime?

1 The King was not very able intellectually and was weak in supporting reforming ministers.

2 The Queen was unpopular.

3 Philosophers wrote about the need for change.

4 There were unfair privileges for the clergy and aristocracy.

5 There were severe financial problems.

6 The American Revolution had encouraged ideas of overthrowing political authority.

7 The middle classes resented their lack of political power.

Least serious ←→ Most serious

Social discontent and economic problems from 1787

REVISED

Social discontent

As well as absolutism and an unfair tax system, the other major source of resentment in French society was corruption at court and in the Church. The system of selling offices (venality) provided income for the monarchy and a bloc of supporters but also led to wasteful corruption and blocked the advancement of those with talent.

There were complaints about the Church. *Curés* (parish priests) complained they were poor because they did not receive the entire tithe. Instead the archbishops, bishops and abbots who often collected it kept most. These higher clergy enjoyed huge incomes which made such positions very desirable. As they were in the personal gift of the King they were secured by court nobles as careers for their younger sons. This led to problems of **absenteeism** and **pluralism**.

The privileges of the court nobles were resented by other nobles. Meanwhile the privileges of the nobility were resented by all the other classes, especially the peasants.

There was a lot of discontent among the middle classes about privilege and the unequal burden of taxation. There was a big expansion of books, newspapers and journals in the eighteenth century and the French middle classes grew in political awareness. There were widespread debating clubs among professionals, both in Paris and the provinces, and an interest in the ideas of the Enlightenment.

Economic problems

The countryside

Conditions across the French countryside varied but foreign travellers, like the Englishman Arthur Young, noted a great deal of rural poverty. Poor harvests between 1770 and 1789 were a major reason for increased hardship. A longer-term issue was land holding. On a man's death, his land was divided equally among his heirs rather than going to the eldest son. The cumulative effect of this was smaller estates. By 1789, roughly a quarter of French farmland was owned by small peasant farmers and much of the rest rented out in small plots. This led to subsistence farming, with no incentive to make improvements in methods or crops. Agricultural problems also adversely affected the woollen industry, which added to rural poverty.

Towns

There was a dramatic growth of towns in the eighteenth century. Towns grew because of the growth in industries (for example, silk in Nîmes) and in foreign trade (for example, ports like Nantes). This growth led to problems and tensions in urban populations.

Most of France's wealthiest and most educated people lived in towns. These were the nobles and bourgeoisie, a few manufacturers and the skilled craftsmen who were organised into guilds. Besides them, there were small property owners, shop-keepers and artisans. However, the majority of the populations of towns were unskilled workers and the urban poor.

Paris had grown in size considerably in the eighteenth century and its poorer districts had become densely populated. Poorer people, including many small traders, craftsmen and labourers, lived in overcrowded and unhealthy conditions. They depended heavily on bread, and any sudden rises in prices would cause hardship and trigger public disorder. Bread riots were a common feature of urban life. There could also be attacks on unpopular employers, as in the riots against the wallpaper manufacturer Réveillon in Paris in April 1789.

Conditions in 1789

The harvest of 1788 was disastrous. The weather in the early months of 1789 was the coldest in living memory and food prices steadily rose to a high point on 14 July 1789.

Mind map

Make a copy of the mind map below and use the information on the opposite page and page 18 to add detail to it, showing how important the social and economic discontent was.

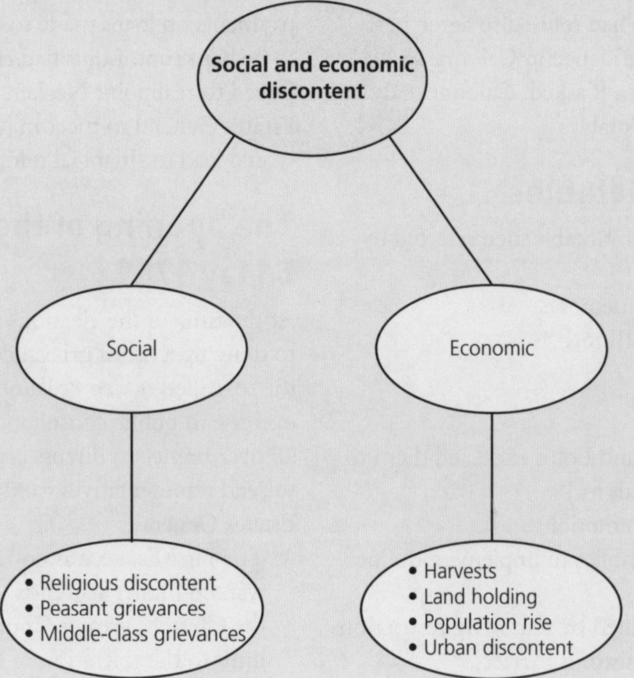

Support your judgement

Read the following sample exam question and two basic judgements. Support the judgement that you agree with most strongly by adding a reason that justifies the judgement.

Tip: Whichever option you choose, you will have to weigh up both sides of the argument. You could use words such as 'whereas' or 'although' in order to help the process of evaluation.

> 'The most serious cause of the French Revolution was economic hardship.' How far do you agree?

Overall, the most serious cause of the Revolution was economic hardship.

____

____

It was not economic but social factors which were the most important reason for the Revolution.

____

____

The Assembly of Notables and political developments 1787 to May 1789

REVISED

In order to collect new taxes, the agreement of the Paris parlement was needed. They had refused to agree new taxes in 1785 and had no confidence in Calonne so he feared they would refuse again if asked. Calonne's advice was to call an Assembly of Notables.

The Assembly of Notables

The Assembly comprised 144 Notable men selected by the King. They included:

- leading members of the parlements
- the seven **Princes of the Blood**
- important nobles
- important churchmen.

They met in February 1787 and Louis expected them to agree with Calonne's proposals for:

- a new land tax with no exemptions
- new elected regional assemblies to implement the new taxes
- the economy to be stimulated by removing restrictions on trade such as internal customs barriers.

However, the Assembly rejected all the government's proposals. The Assembly, once seen simply as an expression of selfish noble opposition to change, came to be seen more as the 'prelude to revolution'. It opposed new taxation without more widespread consultation. The fact that it was summoned at all showed that the situation was very serious and the failure to get agreement weakened the position of the King and his government.

Brienne and aristocratic revolt

After Calonne's failure, Louis appointed Archbishop de Brienne as Controller General. He took revised proposals, again including a new land tax, to the Assembly of Notables. For a second time they refused. Instead, they argued that the approval of the whole French nation was needed for such changes and to obtain this an Estates General should be called.

Louis then dissolved the Assembly and instead presented the proposals to the Paris parlement. They refused to approve them. Louis exiled them to the provincial town of Troyes and used a ***lit de justice*** to force through new taxes. This prompted an aristocratic revolt against absolute monarchy. Nobles and clergy met to discuss how to defend the power of the parlements. This gained much popular support.

In August 1788 the royal treasury had to suspend interest payments on loans made to the state. The crown seemed to be bankrupt. Louis had run out of options. He was forced to reappoint Necker, and agreed to call for an Estates General to meet in May 1789 in the hope that this would lead to financial reform.

The opening of the Estates General, 5 May 1789

At the time of the elections the three estates were asked to draw up a list of grievances and suggestions for reform, the so-called ***cahiers de doléances***. This was a remarkable exercise in public consultation, and meetings were held all over France to discuss grievances. Elections were held to send representatives from the three estates to the new Estates General.

- The First Estate was dominated by parish priests. They wanted higher **stipends**, access to the higher offices of the Church, greater Church control of education and a limit to the toleration of Protestantism.
- The Second Estate was dominated by deputies from long-standing noble families who held conservative views. However, about a third were more liberal in outlook and were willing to give up their financial privileges. They were divided over Third Estate demands for tax reforms and a modern constitution.
- The Third Estate deputies were mainly lawyers, landowners and office holders. Though the Third Estate included the mass of the people, the peasants and workers were not represented proportionate to their numbers.

When the Estates General met at Versailles, Louis failed to put forward a programme of action for discussion. There was no mention of a new constitution, just unspecified talk of fairer taxation. Having asked his subjects what their grievances were, the King offered little in the way of change to deal with them. This proved to be a dangerous misjudgement.

Simple essay style

Below is a sample exam question. Use your own knowledge, information on the opposite page and information from other sections of the book to produce a plan for this question. Choose four general points, and provide three pieces of specific information to support each general point. Once you have planned your essay, write the introduction and conclusion for the essay. The introduction should list the points to be discussed in the essay and outline the line of argument you intend to take. The conclusion should summarise the key points and justify which point was the most important.

Assess the reasons for the crisis in royal authority in 1789.

Develop the detail

a

Below are a sample exam question and a paragraph written in answer to this question. The paragraph contains a limited amount of detail. Annotate the paragraph to add additional detail to the answer.

'Economic and social factors were the most important reason for the French Revolution.' How far do you agree?

The challenge to royal authority came about for many long- and short-term reasons. Though social and economic grievances were important in creating discontent and a demand for change, they were not the most important factors. The years 1787–89 saw a great deal of hardship and high prices, which increased discontent. However, it was not so much social and economic grievances but political factors which led to revolution. The financial crisis more than social and economic grievances was the key factor, but this was linked to other factors such as the state of the economy, resentments in society and the weakness of the King.

The Estates General and events in Paris in 1789

REVISED

The National Assembly, 17 June 1789

The three estates were meant to meet separately. Thus, the nobles, the clergy and the Third Estate would be in separate rooms as they were three distinct classes of society. But the Third Estate argued for voting by head rather than by class. That is, they wanted every member of the Estates General, whether nobleman, clergyman or commoner, voting individually, which would have meant meeting together. The nobility and clergy voted against this. The representatives of the Third Estate were more numerous, so they would be outvoted. Thus there was deadlock because of the lack of agreement about the key issue of how the Estates General would vote.

On 10 June the Third Estate voted to begin verifying deputies' credentials (i.e. whether they were indeed the representatives of their local areas) without the clergy and nobles. This was an essential preliminary to starting discussions. A few clergy joined them. On 17 June the Third Estate voted to call themselves the National Assembly. They claimed to represent the French nation, to speak for the people. Some historians, like William Doyle, see this as the key event of the whole Revolution – the new Assembly claimed its authority not because the King had summoned representatives but because the people had chosen them.

The Tennis Court Oath

Louis tried to regain the initiative by holding a ***séance royale***. Preparations involved closing, without explanation, the Third Estate's (now National Assembly's) meeting room. Angry at what they saw as a despotic act, the deputies moved to a nearby indoor tennis court and swore an oath not to disperse until they had given France a constitution.

At first the King opposed both voting by head and also the new Assembly; but he gave way as popular opinion in Paris turned against the nobility and there were rumours that the Palace of Versailles was going to be invaded by the people. Louis ordered the nobles and remaining clergy to join the Third Estate in the National Assembly. This was a major turning point. The King had been unable or unwilling to control events.

Revolt in Paris – the storming of the Bastille, 14 July 1789

Louis took action to try to restore order in the last week of June, moving more troops into the Paris/Versailles area. It was feared that he was planning to dissolve the National Assembly, using force if necessary.

11 July

With over 20,000 troops in the area, Louis felt strong enough to dismiss the popular minister Necker. This was to spark mass discontent in Paris. The National Assembly was renamed the National Constituent Assembly.

12 July

News of Necker's dismissal spread in Paris and inflamed a tense situation. High food prices had already led to rioting. Necker was seen as the minister to solve the economic crisis. Radical orators like **Desmoulins** claimed that a massacre of the supporters of reform was planned. People armed themselves. There were violent clashes with royal troops. The Paris electors (those who had chosen the representatives of the Estates General) set up a **citizens' militia** to maintain order.

13 July

Barricades were erected to stop any more royal troops entering Paris. In Versailles the Constituent Assembly called for the removal of all troops.

14 July

This was the first ***Journée*** of the Revolution. Parisians seized muskets and cannon from the arsenal, Les Invalides. They then went to the Bastille, a royal fortress and prison, for the gunpowder and cartridges stored there. Troops in the Bastille fired on the crowds and 93 were killed. The people and some members of the ***Garde Française*** stormed the fortress. Launay, the governor, surrendered and was then murdered. The Paris mob – later to be known as the ***sans-culottes*** – had shown their power and neither the new National Assembly nor the King had been able to stop them. Louis had lost control of the armed forces in Paris. An important precedent had been set for political violence achieving results, as the King gave way and made concessions.

15 July

Louis visited the National Constituent Assembly to announce that he was withdrawing all troops from Paris and Versailles. In Paris the electors formed themselves into the new revolutionary council, the **Commune**, and turned the citizens' militia into the National Guard, commanded by Lafayette. They wanted to keep the *sans-culottes* under control.

17 July

Louis now had to share power with the National Assembly. He recalled Necker and visited Paris, where he recognised the legality of the Commune and the National Guard. The Comte d'Artois, Louis' youngest brother, went into exile, as did many other nobles in the following weeks. They believed the royal cause was lost.

Support or challenge?

Below is an exam-style question which asks you how far you agree with a specific statement. Below this is a series of general statements which are relevant to the question. Using your own knowledge and the information on the opposite page, decide which general statements support or challenge the statement in the question and tick the appropriate box.

'The King was to blame for the escalation of the Revolution in 1789.' How far do you agree?

	Support	Challenge
The Third Estate demanded that voting should be by head not order.		
The Third Estate were shut out of their meeting room and went to swear an oath on a nearby tennis court.		
Louis XVI dismissed Necker.		
There were radical orators like Desmoulins who stirred up popular feeling.		
Louis moved troops into the Paris/Versailles region.		
The Estates General declared themselves a National Assembly.		
A Paris Commune and a National Guard were set up.		
The Bastille was stormed on 14 July.		
Louis accepted the National Assembly, the Commune and the National Guard.		

Recommended reading

As this is an area of great historical debate and is part of the topics that could be set for the AS interpretation question, it is worth spending some time studying it in some depth, as it will enhance your understanding of the debates. Below is a list of suggested further reading on this topic.

- Malcolm Crook, *Revolutionary France*, pages 8–15, OUP (2002)
- P.M. Jones, *The French Revolution 1787–1804*, pages 3–32, Longmans Seminar (2003)
- Peter McPhee, *Liberty or Death*, pages 58–80, Yale (2016).
- Dylan Rees and Duncan Townson, *Access to History: France in Revolution*, pages 1–35, Hodder (2001)
- J.M. Roberts, *The French Revolution*, pages 1–20, OUP (1997)
- Sally Waller, *France in Revolution 1776–1830*, pages 1–26, Heinemann (2002)

The Great Fear

REVISED

Developments in the country

Across France, towns and cities copied Paris and set up revolutionary committees and a National Guard to maintain order and to prevent counter-revolution by royalists. The King's intendants abandoned their posts as royal authority collapsed.

The peasantry had not played a very important part in the events of 1788–89 but they had been part of the discussions prior to the calling of the Estates General and their expectations had been raised. The peasant *cahiers* reveal a lot of grievances and these were made worse by the bad harvest of 1788, high food prices and unemployment and lay-offs in the textile trades. Many peasants relied on part-time work and were suffering by the summer of 1789. As authority broke down in Paris and in the regions, so there was a wave of discontent.

Rumours spread that gangs of **brigands** (or criminals) had been hired by fleeing nobles to take revenge by destroying the harvest. Peasants armed themselves and attacked the hated symbols of feudal power. Chateaux and documents recording feudal obligations were burned but few people, nobles or their agents, were killed. Many tithe barns, which held the grain taken by the Church as payment due from the peasants, were attacked. The main unrest was between 20 July and 6 August.

The abolition of feudalism

News of the violence reached the National Assembly deputies. They wanted to crush the rural revolt but did not want to use royal troops in case those troops were used against them. They decided to gain the support of the peasants by giving them what they wanted, the abolition of **feudalism**, though in practice change was slow to take effect.

On 4 August the National Assembly voted for the August Decrees. This was one of the most remarkable debates of the Revolution as the deputies became increasingly enthusiastic about ending privileges.

- Feudal rights over people were abolished.
- Tithes, hunting rights and **seigneurial courts** were abolished.
- All citizens were to be taxed equally.
- All citizens were eligible for any office in Church, state or army.
- Though the nobles were to receive compensation for the loss of their feudal rights, this was later ended in 1793.

The Declaration of the Rights of Man and Citizen, 26 August 1789

The next task facing the deputies was to draft a new constitution. Their first step was the Declaration of the Rights of Man and the Citizen. All citizens were equal. These decrees formally dismantled the Ancien Régime. The Declaration contained very important principles which reflected the thought of the Enlightenment. It began 'Men are born free and remain free and equal in their rights'. This seemed to echo the American Declaration of Independence of 1776, which stated that 'all men were created equal'. The freedoms guaranteed included freedom of speech, opinion, property and justice. The Declaration stated that taxation should be by consent of the governed. Privilege was to be ended, and careers and offices open to all with the necessary talent.

The effects of popular discontent in Paris and other cities, together with the considerable rural unrest of the Great Fear, had acted as a spur to the reforms of the National Assembly to end the Ancien Régime and inaugurate a new **constitutional monarchy** which would recognise the will of the people. The influence of a number of factors can be seen: economic conditions, social unrest, the influence of the American Revolution, the ideas of the Enlightenment, and a weak King. In the country as a whole the people had been consulted in the lead up to the Estates General in an unprecedented way and as a result of the events of 1789 had shown their power and influence.

Develop the detail

a

Below are a sample exam question and a paragraph written in answer to this question. The paragraph contains a limited amount of detail. Annotate the paragraph to add additional detail to the answer.

'The greatest revolutionary changes of 1789 came about because of popular unrest.' How far do you agree?

The storming of the Bastille has been seen as the greatest revolutionary act of 1789 but the biggest impact was made by the widespread peasant disturbances of the summer, which showed the impact of the breakdown of authority in Paris. Though it was important for France to see a new Assembly, the key changes were those made to society when the Assembly abolished feudalism, and the greatest political change followed in August 1789 with the Declaration of the Rights of Man.

Challenge the historian

a

Below is a sample AS exam question including an interpretation written by a historian. You must read the extract, identify the argument in the interpretation, and use your own knowledge to support and provide a counter-argument, challenging the interpretation offered.

'Whatever the mix of motivations in the minds of the deputies, there can be no doubt that it was the "night of 4 August" that tore the ancient regime to shreds. It gave the deputies confidence to hack away at other privileges.'

From: P.M. Jones, *The French Revolution* (2003)

Evaluate the strengths and limitations of this interpretation, making reference to other interpretations that you have studied.

1 What is the view of the interpretation?

____

____

2 What knowledge of your own do you have that supports the interpretation?

____

____

3 What knowledge of your own do you have that challenges the interpretation?

____

____

The October Days

REVISED

The changes voted by the Assembly in August were not legal without the King's acceptance. Louis refused to agree and once again there was a stalemate. Both the King and the Assembly were at Versailles. In Paris there was growing unrest.

The suspensive veto

On 11 September the deputies voted to allow Louis a suspensive **veto**. He could delay laws for up to four years but not veto them completely. They wanted a constitutional monarchy. However, it was not clear that the King would share power. On 14 September he summoned loyal troops from the Flanders Regiment to Paris and they arrived on 28 September.

Unrest in Paris

The flight of many aristocrats from Paris had hit many trades and there was unemployment. Food was not being brought to market by the peasants and bread was in short supply. The middle-class leaders of the Paris Commune and the National Guard established to protect property faced a great deal of revolutionary agitation from orators like **Jean-Paul Marat** stirring up the crowds. The National Guard struggled to maintain order, especially as bread shortages triggered riots. Meanwhile radical journalists like Desmoulins and Marat reported on National Assembly debates and portrayed the supporters of a royal veto as unpatriotic. They advocated direct action by the people. The King was urged to flee but decided to remain at Versailles without any clear plan of either embracing the Revolution or overturning it.

The King insults the Revolution

On 2 October the King seemed to show his disdain for the people by insulting the new revolutionary flag – the Tricolor – at a banquet for the Flanders Regiment. This was seized upon by the radical orators and large crowds, hostile to the King and particularly to the Queen, gathered on 3 October. Marie Antoinette had become particularly unpopular; she was disliked as a foreigner and it was believed that her extravagance had caused financial problems and that she had undue influence over the King.

The march to Versailles

This triggered a violent reaction, a second *Journée*. On 5 October women in Paris seized weapons and marched on Versailles. The National Guard would not stop them. The commander of the National Guard, the Marquis de Lafayette, was ordered by the Commune to follow the marchers.

At Versailles the deputies of the National Assembly had to welcome the marchers. Louis was forced to agree to the August Decrees. Next day the crowd broke into the palace and the Queen was threatened. The National Guard restored order but both the royal family and the deputies were forced to agree to go to Paris.

The King had declined to use force again and returned to Paris from Versailles in a procession accompanied by the National Assembly deputies.

The results of the October Days

Both the National Constituent Assembly and the royal family were now essentially prisoners in the centre of Paris, where they were vulnerable to the power of the crowds. The King had accepted the major changes of August and now was faced with making the experiment of constitutional monarchy work, but he would be under pressure from the Paris mobs.

Introducing an argument

Below are a sample exam question, a list of key points to be made in the answer, and a simple introduction and conclusion for the answer. Read these and then, using the information on the opposite page and pages 20 and 22, rewrite the introduction and the conclusion in order to develop an argument.

'By October 1789 there was little chance that the monarchy would survive.' How far do you agree?

Key points:

- A new National Assembly was formed.
- Violence in the streets of Paris was out of control.
- The King had lost the chance to restore order by force.
- Revolutionary agitators stirred up crowds.
- The Great Fear saw loss of power of nobles.
- Privilege was swept away in the August Decrees.
- The October Days made the King a virtual prisoner.
- The Assembly accepted constitutional monarchy, not a republic.
- King still insisted on the veto and could command troops.

Introduction

To an extent it could be argued that the monarchy would not survive because of the rapid changes that had taken place since May. Radicalism had grown, as had rural discontent. The Assembly had made big changes. The King had had the chance to use troops but had not done so and many of his supporters had fled abroad. The October Days showed his weaknesses.

Conclusion

There was no certainty that the King would be overthrown by October 1789 and it was possible that a constitutional monarchy could have worked. However, the monarchy had been weakened by the events of 1789 and had stood by while there was a lot of violent behaviour.

RAG – Rate the timeline

Below are a sample exam question and a timeline. Read the question, study the timeline and, using three coloured pens, put a Red, Amber or Green star next to the events to show:

- Red: events and policies that have no relevance to the question.
- Amber: events and policies that have some significance to the question.
- Green: events and policies that are directly relevant to the question.

'The most important event in Paris in determining the course of the Revolution in 1789 was the October Days.' How far do you agree?

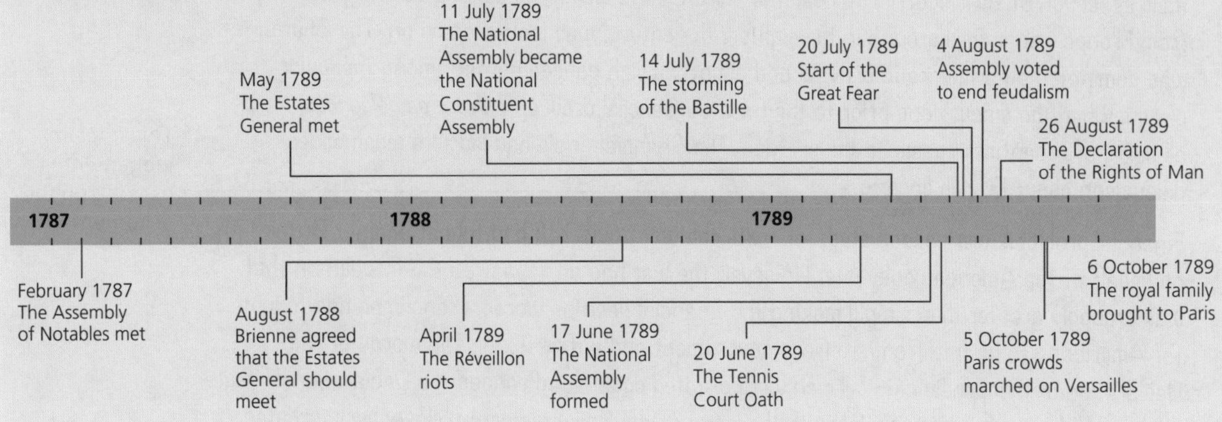

Exam focus

REVISED

Below are a sample exam question and a model answer. Read the question, and then the answer and the comments around it.

Assess the importance of financial problems in bringing about revolution in France in 1789.

The financial situation of the French government by 1789 was one of deep crisis. Because of a series of wars and the inability of Louis XVI to reform the financial system, the deficit had risen to 126 million livres. Normal income could not meet expenditure because of the huge burden of interest payments which by 1788 amounted to 51 per cent of total expenditure. Defence costs took another 36 per cent. Financial problems had become public property with the publication of the royal accounts in 1781. The attempts to deal with the deficit showed the weaknesses of the crown and the power of interests in the state which were opposed to reform. Attempts at financial reform provoked opposition at court, from the parlements and from a special assembly called in 1787 to deal with the crisis. All of this showed the weakness of the King's government. However, the key reason why the financial situation was so important was that the King was persuaded that the way to solve it was to call the Estates General. By August 1786 things were so bad that there was a bankruptcy. The King had rejected calls for the Estates General but could not resist the pressure from the privileged classes to call the old parliament of France rather than simply impose new taxes or end privileges. This decision was crucial in bringing about revolution as it led to widespread discussion of all sorts of grievances prior to the elections and widespread hope for change that the King could not meet.

> The first paragraph deals directly with the issue in the question and makes a clear explanation of the effects of financial problems.

> There is plenty of explanation in the first paragraph but no explicit judgement about the relative importance of financial problems.

However, it could be said that the financial problems were not the main cause of the Revolution but simply showed how important other factors were. It showed that the King and his ministers could not effectively deal with privileges and opposition from selfish interests determined not to give up their special position for the public good. The outdated financial system derived from a respect for privileges enjoyed by the first two estates, the nobles and the clergy. They were exempt from the main possible source of income for the government, the land tax, called the *taille*. This meant an unfair burden on the Third Estate. The financial privileges were only part of the social divisions which were coming to be more and more resented by the Third Estate.

> It takes some time for the answer to give this view, but it is clear.

> Factors are linked here. Weaker answers tend to run through a list of causes without showing links between them.

The whole financial discussion drew attention to privilege. France seemed to be suffering because of the unfair privileges of the few. The Second Estate, the nobles, enjoyed feudal privileges and the right to hold courts in the countryside. They dominated high offices in the army and the Church. Their refusal to reform in the Assembly of Notables was defended by their assertion of their superiority over the Third Estate which, though increasingly wealthy from France's economic growth in the eighteenth century, was looked down on. The Church was dominated by aristocratic bishops and abbots, which caused unrest among the lower clergy. When the discussions prior to the Estates General drew up *cahiers de doléances,* all sorts of resentment came to the surface. The financial crisis had led to a much wider discussion about French society.

> This interim judgement is backing up the argument.

Financial problems were associated, too, with the war Louis XVI had fought against Britain on behalf of the American colonists. However, the war had an impact on the Revolution that was arguably greater than simply making the financial position worse. Frenchmen had fought for Americans to be free from arbitrary government and unfair taxes. The words of the Declaration of Independence – 'all men were created equal' – influenced the Declaration of the Rights of Man and, in conjunction with the ideas of the Enlightenment philosophers, created an atmosphere of questioning of authority that was of much greater importance than the financial crisis.

Other states faced financial problems and other kings were weak, but the combination of political problems with the powerful political ideas from the American War and from the Enlightenment philosophers meant that when the Estates General met in Paris expectations for change were much more extensive than simply wanting to solve the deficit. By 1789 economic hardship with rising prices and poor harvest had given the large Paris population the grounds for discontent. However, it took the excitement of the first meeting of the Estates General since 1614 to turn this discontent from the type of food riot common in the eighteenth century into political disturbance. The storming of the Bastille took place against a background of the Third Estate deputies' frustration that they had not been given the respect due to them because of an outdated social and political system. Thus, the immediate cause of the Revolution was a consequence of financial problems but other causes were much more deep-seated.

The underlying problems of France – the unjust social system, the sufferings of a growing population when harvests were poor, an inefficient government system which a weak King could not use to make necessary reforms – were not new in 1789. The bankruptcy, the sheer size of the deficit and the decision to meet financial problems by summoning the Estates General created the political situation which brought these grievances into widespread public discussion. However, it was the new ideas which were influential among not only the educated class but among an increasing literate urban population that made popular protests into a real revolution. It meant that there was more open criticism, more use of political concepts like the sovereign people (the idea that the people's will gave legitimacy to the rulers and it was they to whom the rulers should be responsible) and more claims that the National Assembly was speaking for 'the people'. This showed how far the Revolution by the time of June 1789 had gone from merely protesting about taxation. Thus it cannot be said that financial problems were the most important factor but they played an important role in the Revolution.

There is rather an abrupt jump between ideas but there is some judgement about relative importance. The argument could be more developed.

Some of the argument in this paragraph is rather telescoped but there is reference back to the issue in the question and factors are linked.

This is a very sophisticated argument which shows the candidate is aware of the significance of the political developments.

There is a clear view taken.

This is a clearly argued and well-focused response. The answer explains the importance of a range of factors and supports the argument with precise, accurate and relevant knowledge. There is evidence of linkage between factors and this is supported in the judgement, suggesting that the argument is logically developed. As a result, it would be placed in the higher levels.

Writing a good opening paragraph

Although the answer scored well, the answer lacks an opening paragraph that outlines the argument and the view of the candidate about the issue in the question. Write an opening paragraph that introduces the line of argument to be pursued and the issues to be discussed.

Exam focus

REVISED

Below are a sample exam question for the AS-Level interpretation question and a model answer. Read the question and then the answer and the comments around it.

> 'The storming of the Bastille was the great psychological and symbolic turning point of the Revolution because it made apparent something that had been true since May: the old absolute monarchy of France was dead.'
>
> J.M. Roberts, *The French Revolution* (1997)
>
> Evaluate the strengths and limitations of this interpretation, making reference to other interpretations that you have studied.

The interpretation is suggesting that the events of 14 July 1789 were the crucial point where the Revolution had developed to such an extent as to change the whole nature of monarchy. There are two aspects in the interpretation. First there were the psychological effects of the triumph of the crowd, showing that traditional authority was weakened and that the people had claimed a right to have a political voice. Secondly the Bastille was symbolic as, though the prison had few inmates, it was an emblem of the power of the old regime in the centre of Paris and, with its fall, the traditional monarchy could be seen to have fallen. After that the change was so radical that eventually the monarchy itself fell and the Revolution would continue to be influenced by riots and direct action.

The response begins by explaining the interpretation; this is crucial as the response, having unpicked the given interpretation, is in a position to examine the strengths and limitations of it. The short extract is analysed thoroughly.

The answer should have placed the given interpretation in context of the wider historical debate about the significance of 14 July and considered the reference to May 1789.

It is true that to some extent the taking of the Bastille was a major turning point. Before this, though, the crowds had been restless. Before this they had not been allowed to exercise such control of the streets while the National Guard and royal forces stood by. They also exacted their revenge with the brutal murder and beheading of Launay, the governor. Instead of the new National Assembly condemning this action and restoring order, there was a tacit assumption that somehow the people had made their voice heard. It set an example for more revolutionary violence culminating in the Terror of 1793–94. The crown had not been strong enough to resist and this too set a precedent and so was a turning point for future developments which led to the October Days, where the royal family was forced to live in Paris, and eventually to the disturbances of 1792 that led to the end of the monarchy. After this it became too hard to use troops and, when Louis did summon loyal troops to Paris in October, he did not use them. The new Assembly could now use the power of the *sans-culottes* for its own ends.

Relevant and accurate own knowledge is directly linked to the given interpretation to show the strengths of the interpretation.

There is further detailed own knowledge linked to the interpretation to further explain its strengths.

Further precise evidence is used to evaluate the interpretation.

However, the interpretation may also overstress the Bastille as a turning point, though it does suggest that the monarchy had already been 'dead' since May. This may be an exaggeration. Simply calling the Estates General did not end the absolute monarchy and there was the option open to take the lead in guiding to reform or suppressing it. However, Louis did not adopt either policy. The result was that the Estates General was dominated by the Third Estate, who claimed legitimacy from June 1789 from the people and then went on to swear an oath in the tennis court at Versailles to create a constitution. The fact that this had been accepted rather than treated as revolution by the King and part of the first two estates was a greater turning point than the disorder at the Bastille. When the Assembly was prepared to stand firm as in the Champs de Mars demonstrations the crowds could be controlled. Napoleon had no difficulty sweeping the streets with his cannon in 1795. The Bastille did not in itself make the mobs undefeatable.

The answer makes it very clear that there are limitations to the interpretation.

A good range of own knowledge is applied and directly linked to the interpretation to illustrate its weaknesses.

This is a strong answer that does explain much of the interpretation and then goes on to use contextual knowledge to show both its strengths and weaknesses. Though the opening might be more developed in terms of establishing a debate, the answer contains analysis at the highest level.

Writing a good opening paragraph

Answers to interpretation questions should start by placing the given interpretation in the wider context of the historical debate about the issue. The first paragraph is clear but could include some explanation of the possible discussion in the wider historical context of 1789. Rewrite the opening paragraph to include an interpretation that argues that the greatest changes had occurred before 14 July 1789 and deals a little more with the reference to May 1789.

2 The Revolution from October 1789 to the Directory, 1795

The reforms in Church and state 1789–91

REVISED

Political, judicial and administrative reforms

Now meeting in Paris, the deputies of the Constituent Assembly brought forward a series of reforms aimed at removing the administrative chaos of the past.

Political and administrative reforms

France was divided into 83 **departments** for elections and local government. These were divided into districts (547), cantons (4,872) and communes (about 44,000) which would be run by elected councils. More power was given to local areas as a safeguard against a royal recovery of power.

The right to vote was given to 'active citizens' – all men over 25 who paid a certain level of tax (4 million). Those ineligible were 'passive citizens' (3 million).

Taxation

Under the new system everyone paid tax. All were liable to pay the land tax and the tax on commercial profits while just 'active citizens' paid a tax on moveable goods such as grain.

Judicial reforms

All previous courts were replaced by a uniform system. There was a **Justice of the Peace** in each canton, trial was by jury, and torture and mutilation were abolished. Justice was free and equal for all.

Church reforms

These were some of the most important changes made by the Revolution.

Civil Constitution of the Clergy, 12 July 1790

Bishops' dioceses were reorganised to coincide with the new 83 departments. All other clerical posts apart from parish priests were removed. Appointment to any clerical post was by election. Many clergy opposed this constitution. Their call for a church synod was denied so they waited for the judgement of the Pope.

Other changes in the Church were:

- All Church property became the property of the state.
- Abuses such as pluralism were abolished.
- The clergy were to be paid by the state instead of collecting the tithe.
- Monastic orders that provided neither education nor charitable work were suppressed.
- Protestants were given full civil rights.

The clergy accepted this although many were unhappy that Catholicism was not made the official religion of France.

The clerical oath, 27 November 1790

The deputies forced the issue by requiring all clergy to take an oath to the constitution. The Pope came out against the reforms. The over 50 per cent who refused to take the oath were called **refractory clergy** and removed from their posts. For devout Catholics like Louis there was a clash between their religion and the Revolution. As a result, a significant number of people now opposed the Revolution.

Economic and social change

The deputies believed in ***laissez faire***. All internal customs barriers were abolished. Under the Loi Le Chapelier, June 1791, the guilds that regulated craft industries and trade unions were banned, and strikes made illegal. This was for the benefit of independent craftsmen and employers, not the very poor.

The deputies saw relief for the poor as the duty of the state. However, little was done. They examined the extent of the problem – almost 2 million people begging – but lacked the finance to do anything.

To finance government, ***assignats*** were introduced, backed by the sale of Church lands. This land sale provided income, created people with a vested interest in supporting the Revolution and left the clergy dependent upon the state for their salaries and thus more likely to be supporters of the new state.

The end of privilege

In June 1790 a law ended the hereditary nobility. The **parlements** were abolished in September 1790.

Delete as applicable

Below are a sample exam question and a paragraph written in answer to this question. Read the paragraph and decide which of the options (in bold) is the most appropriate. Delete the least appropriate options and complete the paragraph by justifying your selection.

How radical were the reforms made by the Constituent Assembly?

The reforms of 1789–91 made **big changes/small changes/some changes** *to* **some/many/a few** *aspects of French life. Local government was changed* **radically/minimally/to some extent**. *Changes to the Church were* **highly significant/of some importance/limited**. *This led to* **some criticism/considerable opposition/no real disagreement**. *The new state* **was very democratic/had some democratic elements/was not at all democratic** *because of the distinction between active and passive citizens. The new justice system was* **important/not very important/insignificant** *in ending the power of the nobles.*

Identify an argument

Below are a series of definitions, a sample exam question and two sample paragraphs. One of the paragraphs achieves a high level because it contains an argument and judgement. The other achieves a lower level because it contains only description and assertion. Using the information from earlier in the book and the opposite page, identify which is which. The mark scheme on page 7 will help you.

- **Description:** a detailed account.
- **Assertion:** a statement of fact or an opinion which is not supported by a reason.
- **Reason:** a statement which explains or justifies something.
- **Argument:** an assertion justified with a reason.
- **Judgement:** an assertion which is supported by a fact or reason.

How far did the people of France benefit from the reforms made by the Constituent Assembly?

Sample 1

There were many changes made in 1789–91 which affected French life and some were beneficial for the people, and some were not. Local government was changed radically by the introduction of new departments, which was important. The Church lost its lands and its privileged position. This helped many people but not all. There was a new taxation system and the economy was affected a lot by the introduction of new paper money called assignats. All privileges were swept away and finally the distinctions between the three orders, or estates, ended, which was beneficial.

Sample 2

The reforms of 1789–91 did meet a lot of the grievances of the people of France but the population as a whole did not benefit as much as the middle classes who had gained more lands and more right to political participation. The restriction on political activity – voting and being deputies – to 'active citizens' based on wealth meant that poorer people were reduced to the status of 'passive citizens', reintroducing class distinction. Also, little was done to relieve poverty, even with 2 million people being reduced to begging. The middle-class deputies also banned trade unions and strikes. The freedom from guild restriction was to help the independent craftsmen not the very poor. For many Catholics, the Church reforms were worrying and many supported priests who did not take the oath to the constitution, dividing France. However, the end of taxation privileges and the power of seigneurial courts did benefit many and many believed that a better, fairer France was emerging from a constitutional monarchy with more power being given to local areas.

The attempts to establish a constitutional monarchy

REVISED

For a constitutional monarchy to work, acceptance by the King was vital and this did not happen. By 1791 he had decided to flee. The other requirement was for moderate political change to be accepted by a majority of the population, but increasingly the political opinions of most of Paris were becoming extreme and moving towards establishing a republic. In opposition were royalist groups who wanted to restore the monarch's authority. Politics became increasingly polarised and there were once again violent scenes.

The King and the flight to Varennes

Initially Louis accepted the Revolution and appeared willing to work towards a constitutional monarchy. Two problems changed his position. First was his religion. Second was the realisation that as a prisoner in Paris his negotiating position was weak.

By 1791 it was obvious that Louis was avoiding hearing mass celebrated by clergy who had sworn the clerical oath. When the royal family tried to leave Paris in April to spend Easter at Saint Cloud, crowds blocked them in. The National Guard ignored orders to clear their way. Louis saw that he was essentially a prisoner and decided to escape.

On 20 June 1791 the royal family left Paris in disguise and travelled east. They were recognised and stopped at Varennes and brought back. The Parisian crowds watched in silence. Louis had left behind a proclamation denouncing the Revolution. The results of this were that:

- Louis had shown he had not understood how popular the changes since 1789 were.
- Many no longer trusted Louis.
- Constitutional monarchy was in doubt.
- Republicanism started to grow.

The political clubs

As the Revolution developed, people met together to discuss politics in a series of political clubs. Some were radical, like the Cordeliers and later the **Jacobins**, while some were moderate, like the Feuillants. Some were monarchists, like the Club Monarchique.

The demonstration at the Champs de Mars, 17 July 1791

The Cordeliers organised a signing ceremony for a republican petition on the Champs de Mars. Roughly 50,000 people attended. The National Guard under the Marquis de Lafayette were called out to maintain order and fired on the crowd. Up to 50 people were killed and the rest dispersed. In the aftermath the Cordeliers Club's leaders, **Brissot** and **Danton**, fled and it was shut down.

The Legislative Assembly

Under the new constitution of 1791 the Legislative Assembly replaced the National Constituent Assembly that had been established on 9 July 1789. Elections took place and on 1 October 1791 the 745 new deputies of the Legislative Assembly met for the first time. They were well-off, as expected from an election system which favoured the wealthy. They were mostly from the bourgeoisie. Few were nobles, most of whom had emigrated or retired to their country estates. A few deputies were clergy.

What were the chances of the constitutional monarchy succeeding?

It may have seemed that there was little chance of success. Many distrusted the King after Varennes. As no former member of the National Constituent Assembly could be a representative in the new Assembly, the new deputies lacked experience. The new government faced bitter divisions in Paris, a King who obviously did not seem to believe in the constitution and had wanted to leave France, and increasing threats from opposition at home and abroad. However, on the positive side, the King did accept the constitution. There were few by October 1791 who supported ending the monarchy. The new Assembly did contain many able men. In addition, the Paris crowds had been controlled by the National Guard in July (see above), which showed that order could be maintained. There had been many changes made to France in 1790–91 which paved the way for a more modern country, so the new constitution might have worked had France been peaceful and stable. But this was not the case.

Support or challenge?

Below is an exam-style question which asks you how far you agree with a specific statement. Below this is a series of general statements which are relevant to the question. Using your own knowledge and the information on the opposite page and page 30, decide which general statements support or challenge the statement in the question and tick the appropriate box.

'The constitutional monarchy established in October 1791 had little chance of success.' How far do you agree?

	Support	Challenge
The King had tried to flee in June 1791.		
Radical political clubs had appeared.		
Popular riots had been suppressed at the Champs de Mars.		
Many nobles and opponents of the Revolution had fled abroad.		
The new electoral system favoured wealthy 'active citizens'.		
The King accepted the new constitution.		
The new Legislative Assembly did contain many talented deputies.		
There had been reforms and changes before 1791.		
Few wanted to end the monarchy.		

Turning assertion into argument

a

Below are a sample question and a series of assertions. Read the exam question and then add a justification to each of the assertions to turn each one into an argument.

'The flight to Varennes ended any hope of a successful constitutional monarchy.' How far do you agree?

The King's flight to Varennes made it impossible for any future constitutional monarchy to work because ...

Though important, the flight to Varennes did not necessarily mean that the constitution of 1791 would fail because ...

The Jacobins and the significance of riots and direct action

REVISED

The crowds played a major part in the development of the Revolution. This was particularly true of Paris, which had over 600,000 inhabitants. The city had expanded and depended on a steady supply of the staple food of the poor – bread. The crowded *faubourgs* (districts) were difficult to control and rioting was common. Eastern districts and the areas to the north of the river were areas prone to riot and in 1789 to political disturbance.

In 1789 political instability coincided with high bread prices and urban distress. The people of Paris had taken part in the consultation exercise that produced the *cahiers* in 1789. They were aware of the high expectations of the Estates General. In April 1789 there were riots about an industrial dispute outside the home of the wallpaper manufacturer Réveillon. There were large crowds at the meeting place in central Paris at the Palais Royal.

Paris had a large number of people who were literate and so could be influenced by increasingly radical newspapers and pamphlets. The crowds were also moved by the orators who demanded change and spoke against privilege.

The first major political riots were over the dismissal of Necker on 11 July and these developed into the storming of the Bastille on 14 July (see page 20). The crowd showed extreme violence in the murder of the governor of the Bastille. The disturbances had destroyed customs posts and the mob attacked prisons and grain hoarders. The so-called *sans-culottes* were not the poorest of the poor but many were small tradesmen and craftsmen. (The name '*sans-culottes*' refers to their wearing the trousers of those who worked for a living, rather than the breeches of the richer people.)

The mob gave the necessary support to the key revolutionary change – the creation of a National Assembly in June 1789 acting in the name of the people. It was this that became the National Constituent Assembly on 9 July and carried out fundamental reforms 1789–91.

Popular action went beyond rioting and was influenced by new political ideas, especially in the Cordeliers Club and by the Jacobins. The *sans-culottes* were represented in the new Commune and the National Guard.

The crowd was influential again in the October Days (see page 24) and after October 1789 the royal family and assembly could be influenced as they were in the centre of Paris.

By July 1791, partly due to the King's flight to Varennes, the Paris crowds were demanding the ending of the monarchy. The demonstrations at the Champs de Mars in July were suppressed but when war began in 1792 (see page 36) the Paris mobs became more threatening and played a major part in the ending of the monarchy. By that time they were allied to a radical political group, the Jacobins.

The Jacobins

This club had its origin in a meeting place of deputies from Brittany in October 1789 in the disused convent of St Jacques – they called themselves the Society of the Friends of the Constitution. Patriotic societies were formed in most French cities in affiliation with the Parisian club. The middle-class members discussed issues raised in the Assembly and aimed to limit the power of the King. Some were more radical and wanted a republic and the club split in 1791. They were divided about war against Austria in 1792 (see page 36). As the Revolution was threatened they became more radical, allying with the *sans-culottes* and demanding an end to the monarchy, more rights for ordinary people and reforms in education. Under **Robespierre**, the Jacobins dominated the government and implemented a radical war policy and new social, religious and economic policies. They were associated with the Terror, which swept away their political enemies.

Developing an argument

a

Below are a sample exam question, a list of key points to be made in the essay, and a paragraph from the essay. Read the question, the key points and the sample paragraph. Using the information from the opposite page and from previous pages in this section, rewrite the paragraph in order to develop an argument. Your paragraph should explain why the factor discussed in the paragraph is either the most significant factor or less significant than another factor.

'Riots and direct actions were the most important driving force of the Revolution 1789–92.' How far do you agree?

Key points:

- Impact of the crowd on 14 July
- Impact of the October Days
- Impact of the fall of monarchy, 1792
- Crowds manipulated by radicals
- Crowds could be controlled – Champs de Mars
- Weakness of crown
- Desire of Assembly for change.

Sample paragraph

Riots and direct actions played a large part in the development of the Revolution from the summer of 1789 through to the end of the monarchy in 1792. Paris had grown in size and its people could not easily be controlled. When there were high prices, the people were particularly susceptible to the influence of radical groups. When the mobs got out of hand, as in the attack on the Bastille, it meant that the Revolution became radical. The crowds played a great role in weakening the authority of the King in October and also in bringing about his fall. Other factors were also important, such as the failure of the crown to control the situation and the ability of orators and radical clubs to use the riots and popular unrest. Many developments in the Revolution were not the result of mob action, such as the changes made by the Constituent Assembly.

Recommended reading

Below is a list of suggested further reading on this topic:

- William Doyle, *Origins of the French Revolution*, pages 166–78, OUP (1980)
- Eric Hazan, *A People's History of the French Revolution*, pages 58–119, Verso Books (2014)
- J.M. Roberts, *The French Revolution*, pages 17–75, OUP (1978)
- Sally Waller, *France in Revolution 1776–1830*, pages 156–67, Heinemann (2002)
- Gwyn Williams, *Artisans and Sans-Culottes*, pages 3–38, Arnold (1968)

The overthrow of the monarchy, 1792

REVISED

The origins and impact of war

In August 1791 Austria and Prussia issued the Pillnitz Declaration threatening combined military intervention in French affairs in support of the King, but did nothing. However, the threat and the presence of *émigré* troops under the Comte d'Artois, Louis' brother, on France's north-eastern frontier made the revolutionaries even more suspicious of the monarchy. They feared counter-revolution and invasion. With the King's support, the government and the Assembly declared war on Austria.

The King clashes with the Assembly

The supporters of war saw it as a chance to make the Revolution more radical. Originally organised by the radical Brissot, they became known as **Girondins**; they seized control of the debates in the Legislative Assembly and were also appointed to the government. The war was opposed by other radicals, especially Robespierre who famously argued that people in other countries would object to 'armed missionaries' of revolution. The Assembly, however, saw refractory clergy and the *émigrés* as counter-revolutionary threats. Two laws were passed. One made not swearing the clerical oath a crime, a conspiracy against the state. The second demanded the confiscation of the property of any *émigrés*, including Louis' brothers, who refused to return to France. Louis vetoed both laws. He also dismissed leading Girondins from his government. He appeared to be obstructing the work of the Legislative Assembly. This increased his unpopularity.

Defeat and extremism

The Revolutionary War began badly. Almost half the officers of the French army had become *émigrés* and its soldiers were demoralised. They were soon retreating, with their generals urging peace talks. This led to mistrust of the King and calls for more revolutionary measures to defeat the enemy.

Sans-culottes and the collapse of the constitutional experiment

The *sans-culottes* dominated Paris and the Paris Commune. They wanted more extreme measures than the Legislative Assembly deputies, such as food price controls and the extension of the vote. Price rises and food shortages triggered riots in early 1792 and made them more militant.

The overthrow of the monarchy, 10 August 1792

On 20 June thousands of *sans-culottes* occupied the royal palace, the Tuileries, and forced Louis to wear a special **Red Cap of Liberty**. The end of the monarchy was in sight.

In July, following the decree of a state of emergency, provincial National Guards (*fédérés*) began to arrive in Paris, joining increased calls for the end of the monarchy. Meanwhile Prussia's army commander threatened to destroy Paris if the royal family were harmed, in the Brunswick Manifesto. This identified Louis with the enemy. He was already unpopular because of his use of the veto and his dismissal of the Girondin ministers. Also Marie Antoinette was believed to be plotting with the Austrians to betray France and was widely unpopular.

On 10 August the Tuileries was attacked and its defenders killed. The royal family took refuge with the Legislative Assembly. The deputies were then forced to hand over Louis, who was imprisoned and the monarchy suspended. They had to agree to a new election, by universal suffrage, of a National Convention that was to draw up a new, more democratic, constitution. For Louis and Marie Antoinette this was to have tragic consequences as both were executed in 1793.

The September massacres

In the aftermath, power was shared between the deputies of the Legislative Assembly, the Revolutionary Commune who controlled Paris and a new body created by them both, the Provisional Executive Council. In another sign of the changed times an Extraordinary Tribunal was set up to try those who had committed counter-revolutionary offences and some people were guillotined.

The Revolutionary War continued to go badly. General Lafayette, after trying to march his army on Paris to end the Revolution, defected to the Austrians. It seemed that the Prussians would capture Paris within weeks. In response, the Commune ordered the arrest of hundreds of suspected counter-revolutionaries. Rumours spread that they planned to escape from prison, massacre the people and surrender Paris to the advancing Prussians. **Jean-Paul Marat** and other Jacobin extremists called for them to be killed. When news of the fall of the fortress of Verdun reached Paris on 2 September, the prisons were broken into. Over the next four days about 1,300 prisoners were murdered. The Revolution had become more violent.

Develop the detail

a

Below are a sample exam question and a paragraph written in answer to this question. The paragraph contains a limited amount of detail. Annotate the paragraph to add additional detail to the answer.

Assess the reasons for the overthrow of the French monarchy in 1792.

There were many long- and short-term causes of the overthrow of the monarchy. The crown had been weakened by the failure either to suppress the Revolution or to take a clear and active lead in establishing a constitutional monarchy. Instead Louis gave the impression that he wanted to undermine the new constitutional arrangements by fleeing in June 1791 and also by his veto. Then he unwisely supported a war and it was the war that more than anything brought about the end of the monarchy.

Simple essay style

Below is a sample exam question. Use your own knowledge, information on the opposite page and information from other sections of the book to produce a plan for this question. Choose four general points, and provide three pieces of specific information to support each general point. Once you have planned your essay, write the introduction and conclusion for the essay. The introduction should list the points to be discussed in the essay and outline the line of argument you intend to take. The conclusion should summarise the key points and justify which point was the most important.

How far was Louis XVI responsible for his own downfall in August 1792?

The Convention and the Terror

REVISED

In 1793 most of Europe turned against France, and there were major risings in the south and west. In response the new National Convention set up the **Committee of Public Safety (CPS)** and the **Committee of General Security (CGS)**.

The Committee of Public Safety

The twelve-man CPS was created on 6 April 1793 to co-ordinate the war effort. It was a war cabinet initially dominated by Danton but coming to be led by more extreme revolutionaries – Robespierre, Couthon and Saint-Just. Carnot, responsible for war strategy and personnel, was behind the decree of 23 August that ordered the *levée en masse*, **conscription**. The CPS also dispatched **representatives on mission** to the armies to improve morale and supervise the generals. In 1793–94, 84 generals were guillotined or shot and 352 were dismissed on suspicion of treachery or defeatism.

Committee of General Security

The CGS was composed of twelve deputies. Their function was to:

- oversee state security including police
- prosecute foreign agents and counterfeiters of *assignats*
- report regularly to the National Convention.

As the threat of invasion and defeat grew, the Convention and its Committees resorted to terror.

The coming of the Terror

As the revolutionary government faced invasion from abroad and opposition from within France, the need for greater control over resources and prices and stricter security measures led to the period known as 'the Terror', with stringent measures being enforced by harsh punishments.

The grain price controls imposed by the National Convention in May 1793 backfired. They led to a growth in a **black market** for grain. Grain supplies fell and food prices rose. Further measures making hoarding grain a capital offence did not work either.

Extremists in Paris, the ***Enragés***, called for higher taxes on the rich, death for hoarders and the arrest of political suspects. They surrounded the National Convention demanding these things and the formation of a *sans-culotte* revolutionary army. The deputies agreed. They also passed a law of general maximum which enforced wage and price controls throughout France.

Added to the threats of external war, internal revolt and *sans-culotte* power, the National Convention deputies faced personal attack. In 1793 two revolutionaries, Lepeletier and Marat, were assassinated. Terror, encouraged by political leaders like Robespierre as a way of getting rid of their enemies and to push the Revolution forward, became the 'order of the day'.

Political terror

On 17 September 1793, the National Convention passed the Law of Suspects. This widened the definition of who was against the Revolution to include royalists, federalists, relations of *émigrés* and anyone without a certificate of loyalty (*civisme*) from their local watch committee. The watch committees were to arrest these suspects and send details of the charge to the Committee of General Security. Prison numbers rose and the Paris Revolutionary Tribunal was divided into four sections, two sitting at any one time, to speed up the trial process.

Executions

The pace of convictions and executions increased. Between March and September 1793, 70 people were guillotined in Paris. Between October and December this rose to 178. In all, to 1794, there were 2,639 death sentences in Paris out of a national total of 16,594. The deaths in Paris were far fewer than in the provinces but the real total of killings was higher than the official figures suggest. In Paris more were killed by mob violence than by the guillotine. The victims of the official terror were not predominantly nobles (8 per cent) or clergy (6 per cent). Middle-class victims made up 14 per cent and ordinary workers or poorer inhabitants made up 72 per cent. Execution for hoarding, illegal trading, desertion, avoiding military service or mere suspicion of wrongdoing was more common than being killed as a result of class war.

Elsewhere, the worst atrocities of the Terror occurred in the suppression of the revolts. In the Vendée region over 8,700 people were executed. Many were guillotined or shot by firing squads; others were deliberately drowned in the River Loire. Such brutality ensured that guerrilla attacks and **scorched earth** reprisals continued into 1794. By the end of the revolt as many as 200,000 people had died. In the south, an example was made of Lyons. The Revolutionary representative Couthon executed 113 rebels in six weeks. This was not enough for the CPS. He was replaced in November by Collot d'Herbois and **Joseph Fouché**. Their revolutionary commission sentenced 1,673 people to death. To speed up the process, and to shock the local population, in December prisoners were placed in front of cannons and mown down by **grapeshot**.

Religious terror

Dechristianisation, the 'religious terror', spread across France by early 1794. This was driven by the *sans-culottes*, the revolutionary armies and some representatives on mission, such as Fouché, rather than the National Convention. Revolutionary hatred of the Catholic Church led to the removal of thousands of priests and the closure of churches. Robespierre disliked the attacks and wanted to form a new revolutionary religion.

Spectrum of importance

a

Below are a question and a list of general points which could be used to answer the question. Use your own knowledge and information on the opposite page to reach a judgement about the importance of these general points to the question posed. Write numbers on the spectrum below to indicate their relative importance. Having done this, write a brief justification of your placement, explaining why some of these factors are more important than others. The resulting diagram could form the basis of an essay plan.

'The main reason for the Terror of 1793–94 was war.' How far do you agree?

1 Robespierre wanted to overthrow his political enemies.
2 There was a real fear of conspiracy.
3 There was pressure from the Paris *sans-culottes*.
4 There was the need to stop counter-revolution in the provinces.
5 France needed total discipline to fight foreign enemies.
6 The ruling group believed in revolutionary purity and virtue at all costs.
7 Two revolutionary leaders were assassinated.

Least important reason ←→ Most important reason

Turning assertion into argument

a

Below are a sample question and some assertions. Read the exam question and then add a justification to each of the assertions to turn each into an argument.

'Foreign war was the main reason for the Terror of 1793-94'. How far do you agree?

The war was the key factor in bringing about the Terror because ...

Counter Revolution was more important than war in bringing about the Terror because ...

The rise of Robespierre

REVISED

A lawyer from Arras, Robespierre first came to national attention in 1789 when he was elected as a deputy to the Estates General. He became well known for his radical views, his belief in democracy and his opposition to capital punishment and slavery. Robespierre rose to prominence in the Jacobin Club and gained a reputation as an incorruptible politician. On 5 September 1792 he was elected to the National Convention and became a leader of the **Montagnard** faction.

The struggle for power

There was a struggle for power between the Montagnards and the less extreme Girondin group. Robespierre had the support of the *sans-culottes* who wanted control of bread prices and harsh measures against enemies of the Revolution.

The Journée of 2 June 1793

At the Jacobin Club Robespierre called for an insurrection against 'corrupt deputies'. On 2 June the National Convention was surrounded by National Guards demanding the arrest of 29 Girondins. The deputies were forced to agree.

The trial of 21 of the Girondins began on 24 October 1793. The Girondins were convicted and guillotined on 31 October. Other prominent revolutionaries followed them.

The dictatorship of the CPS under Robespierre

By the end of 1793 the Jacobin government had succeeded. Revolts had been defeated and foreign troops driven from France. It was then possible for Robespierre and the CPS to control the *sans-culottes*. He had used them in his rise to power but no stable government could be dependent on them. In September the National Convention decreed that the sections of the Paris Commune should meet only twice a week. This limited *sans-culotte* ability to organise. In October the deputies passed a decree that suspended the constitution with its one-man-one-vote system.

The Law of Frimaire, 4 December 1793

This established revolutionary government, which:

- confirmed that the CGS and the CPS had full executive powers including control of local government, which enabled them to break the power of the *sans-culottes* in the Paris Commune
- disbanded all revolutionary armies except that in Paris.

This Jacobin government was now a dictatorship with Robespierre as the dominant figure.

Challenges to the CPS

In 1794 the CPS faced two challenges: from the **Indulgents**, a faction led by Danton, who campaigned to end the Terror, and from the Hébertists, followers of **Hébert**, who wanted more Terror. First Robespierre moved against the Hébertists, who were arrested and executed. Danton and the Indulgents were then removed, convicted and guillotined the next day, 5 April 1794.

The Great Terror

During the Great Terror, 10 June to 27 July, the revolutionaries saw conspiracy everywhere. Following Danton's fall no one dared challenge the CPS. Its eleven surviving members carried on with centralising control and repression. They passed new laws:

- **Law on General Police** – allowed the CPS to set up a police bureau to catch counter-revolutionaries and to recruit agents to identify suspects all over France. Enforced by Saint-Just, and later Robespierre, it sent suspects, mostly nobles and clergy suspected of counter-revolutionary conspiracy, and ex-Hébertists, to the Revolutionary Tribunal.
- **Law of 19 Floreal** – gave the Paris Revolutionary Tribunal jurisdiction over all counter-revolutionary offences.
- **Law of Prairial, 10 June 1794** – widened the definition of political crimes so that almost anyone could be included. Drafted by Robespierre and Couthon, this law made guilty verdicts by juries more likely as it abolished both defence counsels and public cross-examination of defendants. Defence witnesses did not have to be heard nor evidence produced. The only verdicts the Tribunal could reach were death or acquittal. The impact of the law was to drop the acquittal rate to just 20 per cent while the use of batch trials (groups of defendants tried together on the same charge) speeded things up.

Robespierre and religion

Robespierre disliked attacks on religion and the radical dechristianisation and believed in a God (the Supreme Being) and the immortality of the soul. He linked these beliefs to the promotion of republican virtue by setting up the Cult of the Supreme Being in May 1794. There were to be public festivals to recognise this God and to link this religion to liberty and republicanism with special ceremonies and images. It pleased few.

Turning assertion into argument

Below are a sample question and a series of assertions. Read the exam question and then add a justification to each of the assertions to turn them into an argument.

Assess the reasons for the rise of Robespierre.

Robespierre depended heavily on support of the Paris *sans-culottes* because ...

____

____

However, this would not have been possible if circumstances had not been favourable because ...

____

____

A major reason was the fall of Danton because ...

____

____

Spot the mistake

a

Below are a sample exam question and a paragraph written in answer to this question. Why does this paragraph not get into Level 3? Once you have identified the mistake, rewrite the paragraph so that it displays the qualities of at least a Level 3. The mark scheme on page 7 will help you.

How dictatorial was the rule of Robespierre?

Robespierre was a leading Jacobin and he rose because of his support for the Revolution and its enemies and because of the demonstrations of 23 June 1793. He was a leading member of the Committee of Public Safety and an ardent believer in defending the Revolution by encouraging 'public virtue' and loyalty to revolutionary ideas. He destroyed those who opposed him almost as a matter of public duty rather than for personal reasons and could only have risen to power because of war and counter-revolution.

The fall of Robespierre and the establishment of the Thermidorian regime

REVISED

Thermidor

The wartime dictatorship of Robespierre and the Committees was becoming too extreme, especially as the French armies were no longer threatened and Robespierre's policies, such as the Cult of the Supreme Being, seemed more and more eccentric. In July 1794 Robespierre was overthrown and the Terror came to an abrupt end in the bloodbath of Thermidor, a coup named after the month in the new revolutionary calendar that replaced July. Robespierre tried to address the National Convention but was shouted down. The day before his arrest, in a long speech, Robespierre had said there was a 'conspiracy against public liberty' that involved deputies, the CGS and even members of the CPS. He promised to name those involved. Moderates and extremists alike feared it might be them so they combined against Robespierre, accusing him of dictatorship.

Robespierre and his close associates on the CPS, Couthon and Saint-Just, were arrested. Later that day they escaped and went to the Paris Commune to try to rally their supporters against those of the National Convention. They failed and were rearrested. Now Robespierre and his supporters, including the entire Paris Commune, had become armed rebels and that afternoon, after simply being identified, they were guillotined.

Robespierre fell because he had:

- been ill and had withdrawn from the CPS and the National Convention
- had long-standing quarrels with the supporters of dechristianisation and the more extreme supporters of the Terror, notably Fouché
- become a figure of ridicule over his recent role as high priest of the Cult of the Supreme Being
- lost *sans-culotte* support because of his attacks on the Hébertists and threatened wage reductions
- given other revolutionaries reason to fear that he might accuse them of conspiracy.

After the events of Thermidor the surviving members of the CPS tried to continue the Terror but the deputies of the National Convention reasserted their control to end it.

The Thermidorian reaction

The Thermidorians were the men who overthrew Robespierre. They included the surviving members of the CPS and the CGS, ex-supporters of the Terror, and the deputies of the National Convention. Robespierre and his associates were labelled as **Terrorists** and blamed for the Terror. Some who had not died with him at Thermidor were also guillotined.

The deputies of the National Convention moved to end the Terror and reverse the process of centralisation by:

- ensuring that the membership of the CPS and CGS was changed frequently
- setting up new committees to share government responsibilities
- reorganising the Revolutionary Tribunal
- repealing the Law of Prairial
- releasing all suspects from prison
- abolishing the Paris Commune
- closing the Jacobin Club.

It also established freedom of worship for all religions.

The White Terror

In Paris, gangs attacked former Jacobins, militants and *sans-culottes*. In the provinces the violence was worse. In the south massacres and street murders cost as many as 2,000 lives in 1795. In the west **guerrilla warfare** flared again in the Vendée with the **Chouan** movement.

The 1795 Parisian risings

The Thermidorians abolished price controls in 1794. This led to a fall in the value of the *assignat* and high inflation. At the same time a harsh winter led to food shortages. There was more unrest named, like Thermidor, after the new names of the months in which it took place according to the revolutionary calendar.

Germinal, 1 April 1795

The shortages led to a huge demonstration in Paris. The National Guard stayed loyal to the Convention and the demonstrators were dispersed. In the aftermath some ex-Terrorists were exiled to the **'dry guillotine'** of Guiana.

Prairial, 20–22 May 1795

This *Journée* was serious as some demonstrators were armed and some National Guards joined them. Loyal army units arrived and they were able to regain control. Some of the demonstration leaders were arrested, tried and executed, and others imprisoned. Thousands were disarmed and the power of the *sans-culottes* was finally broken.

Complete the paragraph

a

Below are a sample exam question and a paragraph written in answer to this question. The paragraph contains a point and specific examples, but lacks a concluding explanatory link back to the question. Using the information from the opposite page, complete the paragraph by adding this link in the space provided.

How stable was the Thermidorian regime established in 1794?

The Thermidorian regime was established as a result of a violent coup against extremists. Though it was a relief to many in the Convention, as well as in the country as a whole, that the power of Robespierre and the Terrorists had been broken, France still faced many problems. Though no longer as dangerous as at the height of the Terror, France still faced foreign opposition and internal rebellion. There were ongoing financial problems and there were risings not only in the provinces but also in Paris itself.

Develop the detail

a

Below are a sample exam question and a paragraph written in answer to this question. The paragraph contains a limited amount of detail. Annotate the paragraph to add additional detail to the answer.

Assess the reasons for the fall of Robespierre.

Robespierre had become increasingly extreme and out of touch with not only the Convention but also his own supporters. The emergency conditions which had justified the imposition of the Terror were not so pressing by the time of Thermidor. Also Robespierre had lost some of his political skill and allowed himself to be isolated. His religious policies seemed to many to be absurd and he seemed to be motivated by an ever-increasing desire for deaths in pursuit of virtue and purity.

The establishment of the Directory

REVISED

The constitution

The Thermidorians produced a new constitution in 1795. It was designed to prevent a return to a monarchy or to a dictatorship like that of the CPS and to control by the common people, the *sans-culottes*. France was to be ruled by a new governing committee of five, called the Directory, who were:

- chosen by the Council of Ancients (see below) from a list drawn up by the Five Hundred
- to hold office for five years.

One was chosen by lot to retire each year.

The National Convention (Legislature) was replaced by two Councils:

Council of Five Hundred	Council of Ancients
• All members had to be over 30 • Initiated legislation	• All 250 members had to be over 40 • Approved or rejected legislation

Annual elections for both changed one-third of members each year.

There was an indirect system of elections. All males over 21 who paid direct taxes (approximately 5.5 million men) could vote for a special elite group called electors. These electors, rich men who paid high taxes (approximately 30,000), voted for Council members.

The constitution had several weaknesses:

- Yearly elections led to instability.
- There was no mechanism to resolve disputes between the Directors and the two Councils. This could, and did, lead to stalemate and inaction.

Economic and financial problems and policies

The Directory faced serious economic and financial problems.

Economic problems

The Directory first tried to solve the problem of inflation by issuing a new paper currency. When that failed and had to be withdrawn, metal coins became the legal currency. As there were not enough coins in circulation, trade and commerce were hindered. **Deflation** was the result. This failure made the Directory unpopular with all sections of society.

Financial problems

The Directory was more successful with solving the problem of government finances. In September 1797 two-thirds of the national debt was written off through the issue of special bonds to government creditors. These bonds could be used to buy national property, i.e. property confiscated from the crown, the Church and others. However, these bonds fell in value until they became worthless. This resulted in a loss by those who had lent to the state. It was called 'the bankruptcy of two-thirds'. The debt was now gone but at the cost of the Directory losing the support of all those original government creditors.

For government income the Directory relied in part on the profits of war, plunder taken from captured territories in Germany and Italy. This allowed the Directory to function but at the cost of greater reliance on the army and on an aggressive war policy. Problems remained with hostility from the *émigrés* who had fled from France to stir up opposition and also from hostile foreign powers in the Second Coalition against France (see page 54).

The lasting solution was provided by the finance minister, Vincent Ramel. In 1798 he reformed the tax system by:

- introducing four new direct taxes; the tax on windows and doors hit the rich hardest
- reintroducing an indirect tax, the octrois, a tax on goods entering towns
- making tax collection more efficient.

The effect of these policies was to balance government finances, but at the cost of alienating those sections of society adversely affected by the bankruptcy and new taxes.

Support or challenge?

Below is an exam-style question which asks you how far you agree with a specific statement. Below this is a series of general statements which are relevant to the question. Using your own knowledge and the information on the opposite page and page 42, decide which general statements support or challenge the statement in the question and tick the appropriate box.

'The Directory was successful in establishing a new government and bringing financial stability in 1795–98.' How far do you agree?

	Support	Challenge
The early years were characterised by rising prices.		
This was followed by deflation.		
There was reform of the tax system in 1798.		
The new constitution had two Councils and was designed to restrict the power of the *sans-culottes* and to prevent a restoration of the monarchy.		
Limited numbers of people could vote.		
In 1797 there was the bankruptcy of two-thirds.		
Foreign successes by French armies led to money coming into France as plunder.		
The Terror ended.		

Introducing an argument

a

Below are a sample exam question, a list of key points to be made in the answer, and a simple introduction and conclusion for the answer. Read these and then, using the information on the opposite page and pages 40 and 42, rewrite the introduction and the conclusion in order to develop an argument.

How serious were the problems facing the Directory before 1799?

Key points:

- Contrast with Terror
- Constitution
- Economic problems
- Financial changes
- Political unrest
- Reliance on army and conquest.

Introduction

There were many problems facing the Directory as the leaders had to draft a constitution which kept a balance between an element of democracy and a strong executive. The wars had also made the financial situation worse and the reliance on paper money based on confiscated Church lands (*assignats*) had led to inflation. The internal disturbances that had characterised much of the Revolution continued. The financial situation required a reordering of national finances which was achieved in 1798.

Conclusion

Thus there were long-term problems inherited from the revolutionary period which included the opposition from *émigrés*, internal revolts and the Second Coalition, and short-term problems arising from the deflation which resulted from trying to control rising prices and implementing financial reforms. The basic constitution and structure had some limitations, too, in that relatively few people voted and power was concentrated in the hands of the Directors.

Exam focus

REVISED

Below are a sample exam question and a model answer. Read the question and then the answer and the comments around it.

'Louis XVI was responsible for the fall of the monarchy in 1792.' How far do you agree?

The constitutional monarchy, which began in October 1791, was already likely to fail. This partly due to the attitude of Louis XVI and partly to the circumstances which followed the revolutionary events of 1789. Its failure was confirmed by the strains of a war which Louis XVI actively promoted and his failure to compromise and gain the trust of his ministers and the Assembly. However, though Louis played into the hands of his enemies, he was not fully responsible for the extremism that emerged in 1792 and the alliance of the radical republicans with the *sans-culottes*. He had allowed a deadly situation to emerge and must bear a share of the responsibility for the fall of the monarchy, but the violence of the opposition, stirred by defeats in war, created a situation which he could not control.

The introduction establishes a clear line of argument, which focuses directly on the question. The argument put forward in the opening paragraph is developed throughout the essay and the conclusion reinforces the points made at the start.

The King had alienated many in the Assembly by his refusal to give up his suspensive veto and his opposition to the Civil Constitution of the Clergy. However, the decision to flee the capital in June 1791 undermined his reputation and authority. It seemed that the King wished to flee to the enemies of the Revolution and betray his own people. However, the King had accepted the idea of a constitutional monarchy. He had not used opportunities to suppress the Revolution. The flight was not only inconsistent with his declarations but it was also seriously mismanaged. The incompetence which he had shown in many aspects of government was confirmed by his inability to organise an escape and compromising documents left behind made him seem an enemy of change. His return was a humiliation but as, by June 1791, there was no consensus for deposing the King, there was a tacit agreement to carry on with the new constitution. However, with *émigrés* in the neighbouring territories raising forces and the obvious hostility of the other monarchs of Europe, the episode of the flight had made for instability and was a major reason why Louis could be seen to be responsible for his own downfall.

The opening sentence could be stronger and more directly focused on and linked to the actual question, but there is an argument in the next part which suggests Louis was to blame.

With the establishment of the new constitution there were hopes that France had made a new beginning. The reforms of 1789–90 had led to reform and modernisation and the Legislative Assembly had a new membership, including some able men. However, there were circumstances which Louis was not able to control which undermined his chances of evolving into a constitutional monarch. The first was the development of more extreme political clubs in Paris and the provinces whose members were prepared to use ongoing discontent to end the monarchy and install a more radical and democratic republic. This discontent would have been challenging in a time of peace. However, there were internal and external threats to the Revolution which led to calls for war. These circumstances were not in Louis' control but he took the fateful decision to encourage foreign war and to that extent ensured his own downfall.

The discussion about the situation after Varennes is balanced – the essay is not arguing that Louis was totally to blame and the context is considered.

The wars that began in April 1792 were actively supported by a powerful faction, led by Brissot, though opposed by other radical groups fearing they would give the King the chance to launch a counter-revolution. Louis supported war, outwardly showing himself as a unifying influence for France against its external enemies and showing his support for the new regime. However, part of the calculation was that if the French revolutionary armies lost then he would be restored to full power by foreign invasion. This was a dangerous and short-sighted policy. Losses would give his enemies the excuse to accuse him of disloyalty, to associate

The argument about the link between the King and other elements is continued.

Marie Antoinette with betrayal and prove that Louis had agreed to war only to restore his position. French victories might equally inspire people to spread the Revolution and to take it to a new stage – a republic.

This highly dangerous strategy proved to be fatal to the monarchy. The initial enthusiasm for war gave way to panic when the professional armies of Austria and Prussia proved too strong for the hastily raised forces of France. Matters were made worse when generals deserted, indicating that the 'establishment' was fundamentally disloyal. Accusations of treason and betrayal of plans to the enemy were rife and matters were made considerably worse by the threats made by the Prussian commander Brunswick to raze Paris to the ground if the royal family was threatened.

What occurred now was a re-emergence of the mob activities that had been so destructive and threatening before. In themselves they were out of the control of the King. However, he had ignored the possibility of defeats encouraging the hysteria and paranoia that had been evident when mobs feared a counter-revolution. The *sans-culottes* were encouraged by the radical parties in Paris which had gained support when they could claim that they needed to save the Revolution. Again these radicals developed independently of any royal action but they were able to exploit the King's past mistakes – from Louis' mishandling of the Estates General in 1789 to the flight to Varennes. These were complained of in the streets and eventually became accusations at the King's trial.

The key event which ended the monarchy was the demonstration of 10 August 1792. By then the capital was out of control and even at the end the King showed weakness. He ordered his guards to cease firing on the crowds, which resulted in their massacre. But the alliance of Jacobins, the Paris mob and an influx of revolutionary troops from the south proved too much. The King's supporters fled and the Assembly abolished the monarchy on 21 September. Circumstances had become extreme but the King lacked the courage to maintain himself against his enemies.

Without the defeats in war which led to the danger of foreign invasion and the heightened atmosphere following the Brunswick manifesto, the violent events of 10 August 1792 would not have been acceptable. However, the King had helped to create the conditions of his own downfall. He lost the chance to co-operate with the Girondins without being able to suppress rebellion and even at the very end lacked firmness. However, the extreme violence of the September massacres was indicative of the rise in extremism that he was only partly responsible for, so while the statement that he was responsible for the fall of the monarchy is justified to an extent it cannot be the full explanation.

An argument about the war is put forward and this is built on in the remainder of the paragraph. There is analysis of the dangers that the King's support for war gave rise to.

The paragraph about the war is rather too descriptive and the question is rather lost sight of here.

The paragraph links the developing radicalism with the King's own mistakes and offers a rather harsh judgement about the King.

The final paragraph comes back to the thesis proposed in the opening.

Throughout the essay the answer is well supported by appropriate and accurate knowledge of complex events. Significantly the evidence is used most of the time to support the argument and not simply to describe the events. The opening sentences could have been better linked to the actual question. However, a clear view is taken and by and large followed through. The answer does show judgement in terms of the question, but this could be more fully developed and consistent. The conclusion supports the line of argument adopted in the rest of the essay. Despite some shortcomings, the answer is focused and does analyse the main issues to reach a balanced judgement and therefore would reach the higher levels.

Making a judgement

In order to reach the very top level candidates need to reach judgements about the issue they are considering in relation to the question. Identify the paragraphs where the candidate has successfully done this and those where a judgement is either absent or is not developed. In the latter case write a couple of sentences for each of the paragraphs so that a judgement based on the argument is reached.

Exam focus

REVISED

Below are a sample short-answer question and model answer. Read the question and then the answer and the comments around it.

Which was of greater importance in bringing about the fall of Robespierre and the establishment of the Thermidorian regime?

i The Cult of the Supreme Being

ii The loss of support of the sans-culottes

Explain your answer with reference to both (i) and (ii).

Robespierre's religious policy seemed out of touch with the ideas of many fellow Jacobins and members of the Convention while not gaining him popular support and helping to isolate him and make it easier to overthrow his power.

Robespierre wanted to unite Frenchmen in a new religion and brought in the Cult of the Supreme Being in 1794 along with special ceremonies to worship an all-powerful creator not linked to any particular religious denomination. This seemed sacrilegious to loyal Catholics while to Robespierre's republican supporters it seemed that Robespierre was trying to reintroduce Christianity, which went against the anti-clericalism of many fellow Jacobins. The ceremonies seemed eccentric and indicative that Robespierre was moving the Revolution away from its original ideas and showed that he was becoming too dictatorial and powerful in wanting to shape people's beliefs.

The loss of support of the *sans-culottes* was vital because when Robespierre was overthrown the crowds did not come out to support him. The *sans-culottes* had resented the destruction of the radical Hébert and his supporters by the Committee of Public Safety and greater controls on popular movements. It was their power which had brought about the end of the monarchy and they had supported the Terror, but they had come to distrust Robespierre, particularly with rising inflation and maximum prices. With economic hardship and an end to the obvious threat from invasion and counter-revolution, together with large numbers of quite ordinary people being victims of the Terror, the key support that Robespierre needed when his enemies turned against him was not there.

Although both factors were important, the most significant was the ending of the support of the *sans-culottes*. The Cult of the Supreme Being was more significant in worrying people in rural areas than in Paris itself. Robespierre's supporters were more worried about the threat of the Terror falling on them than about the bizarre ceremonies he devised. Also Robespierre's influence had depended heavily on the support of the people of Paris and his ability to use this. The plotters of Thermidor might not have acted had they feared a massive popular uprising. The arrest of Robespierre took place without resistance. This cannot be explained by the unease felt by anti-clericals about Robespierre's religious ideas, but more by the failure to mobilise public sympathy.

The significance of the Cult is clearly explained in the first paragraph.

The response offers a number of reasons why the Cult was important and these are fully expanded and developed.

The importance of the loss of support is explained.

Reasons are given for the loss of the *sans-culottes'* support which might be linked to its importance. These are developed, with good, detailed knowledge.

There is some explanation of the importance.

A clear view as to the most important factor is identified.

The judgement is further developed and there is a comparison between the two factors.

The response analyses and evaluates both factors. The supporting knowledge is detailed and accurate and this allows a developed judgement to be reached based on the evidence in the two main paragraphs. The answer would therefore be placed in the higher levels.

Making a judgement

In order to reach the higher levels you must reach a judgement as to which factor was the more important. This response argues that it was the loss of the *sans-culottes*' support. Use the information in the answer to rewrite the conclusion to argue that the cult of the Supreme Being was more important.

3 Napoleon Bonaparte to 1807

Napoleon's background, character and military leadership

REVISED

Napoleon Bonaparte was born in Corsica in 1769, one year after it became part of France. Born into a minor aristocratic family, he was sent to France for his education. He entered the École Militaire in Paris in 1784 and was its first Corsican graduate. The family relied on the patronage of the French governor to support Napoleon's training in France. The military school was usually reserved for French cadets of good families and Napoleon, with his Corsican accent and Italianate appearance, was an outsider. Instead of being commissioned in a cavalry regiment he became a lieutenant of artillery. A lonely, withdrawn youth, he studied and read widely – military history and the theorists of the eighteenth century, classics and mathematics.

The Revolution

In 1789 Napoleon returned to Corsica and became involved in revolutionary politics. However, this brought him into conflict with the veteran Corsican nationalist leader Paoli and in 1793 the entire Bonaparte clan had to flee to France.

Bonaparte had become a Jacobin supporter and had established a friendship with Robespierre's brother, Augustin, and a fellow Corsican Jacobin, Salcetti. These connections gave him his first chance and he took a leading role in the battle to expel British forces from the key naval base at Toulon, which they had occupied in 1793.

First fame

Bonaparte showed his battlefield skills and made good use of his artillery knowledge. The defeat of the British won him fame and he was put in charge of the coastal defences on the Mediterranean. However, with the fall of the Jacobins and his refusal to take a demotion by accepting a post in the army fighting in the civil war in the Vendée (see page 38), his career slumped.

13 Vendémiaire

Once again political connections saved Napoleon's career. In October 1795 the Convention was under threat from royalist mobs in Paris and Bonaparte's political radicalism and knowledge of artillery led him to be put in charge of suppressing the crowds. He brought up artillery and fired at the protesters at close range. This 'Whiff of Grapeshot' on 13 Vendémiaire (October) 1795 made him a candidate for promotion and helped him to get the key opportunity in his career, commanding the French army stationed in Northern Italy in 1795 (the Army of Italy).

Marriage

Marie-Josephe-Rose de Tascher de la Pagerie, known as Joséphine, had been born in Martinique and at sixteen had had an arranged marriage with an aristocrat, Alexandre de Beauharnais. They both were arrested during the Terror and he was executed. Napoleon was taken with her sexual and social sophistication and they began an affair. They were married in March 1796.

Character and influences

Napoleon was an outsider. His Corsican background dominated his career and he relied on influential patrons and then promoted his own family. He absorbed the new ideas of his age about military organisation, the use of artillery, state-building, finance and law, and had the sharpness of mind to extract their essence and see how to put them into practice. He admired the principles of the Revolution but despised the common people. Firing his cannon into the Paris crowds, killing prisoners in the Middle East, destroying enemy troops in retreat with cannon and heavy losses of his own men did not appear to worry him. Above all, he was supremely confident that his destiny was to command, first armies then nations. He talked of his 'star' guiding him to ever-increasing glory.

However, the Corsican heritage was only part of his character. The other part was formed by his study of Enlightenment thinkers and reformers and his admiration for Enlightened despots like Frederick the Great and also the Revolution. His wedding gift to Joséphine was a medallion with two words – not 'With Love', but 'To Destiny'.

Develop the detail

Below are a sample exam question and a paragraph written in answer to this question. The paragraph contains a limited amount of detail. Annotate the paragraph to add additional detail to the answer.

How much did Napoleon's rise in the 1790s depend on his character?

Napoleon had a determined character, forged both in Corsica and on the battlefields of the revolutionary wars. He did not have the privileges of his fellow cadets in military training and was always an outsider. He was prepared to make the most of any situation which allowed him to gain more power and influence, and thought that he was destined for fame and glory. However, it was not entirely due to his own character and abilities that he was able to rise to prominence. The circumstances were very favourable.

Support your judgement

a

Read the following sample exam question and two basic judgements. Support the judgement that you agree with most strongly by adding a reason that justifies the judgement.
Tip: Whichever option you choose you will have to weigh up both sides of the argument. You could use words such as 'whereas' or 'although' in order to help the process of evaluation.

'Napoleon rose to prominence through his ruthlessness and ambition.' How far do you agree?

Ruthlessness and overwhelming ambition characterised the rise of Napoleon.

Ruthlessness and ambition alone could not have led to the rise to prominence of Napoleon.

Napoleon's military leadership to 1799

REVISED

Initial success

At the siege of Toulon in 1793, as commander of the artillery, Napoleon devised the plan which drove the British navy out. This won him promotion to brigadier general in charge of the artillery of the French Army of Italy. It also led to him being used by the Directory government to protect them against the Paris mobs. The vigorous war minister Lazare Carnot picked out Bonaparte as a successful commander and appointed him to head the Army of Italy.

Italian campaign, 1796–97

Napoleon fought an unexpectedly successful campaign in Italy. France had been fighting the Austrians and their allies in Italy with little success. He took over a small army and with his charismatic leadership won a series of victories.

Though the Army of Italy was not as weak as has been suggested, it had not been well led or active and Bonaparte gave it new energy. By rapid advances and surprise attacks he defeated the northern Italian state of Piedmont in two weeks. He then led a series of victories against the Austrians culminating in the Battle of Rivoli in January 1797. Napoleon seemed to be a new kind of commander. He inspired the assault on a defended bridge at the Battle of Lodi, 10 May 1796. He abandoned the slow-moving mass infantry, common in the eighteenth century, for fast-moving marches in which his troops lived off the land rather than relying on supply depots or slow baggage trains. He also understood how to use the better artillery that the French armouries were able to produce.

A French advance towards Vienna was a real threat and after Bonaparte won a victory only 100 kilometres from the city, Austria sued for peace. Bonaparte himself negotiated the Treaty of Campo Formio which gave France the Austrian Netherlands (Belgium) and much of Northern Italy. New territories of Nice and Savoy were annexed and two satellites – the Cisalpine and Ligurian Republics – set up. He then took his forces into the independent state of Venice. Many of his later tactics were developed in this highly successful campaign, such as:

- maintaining high morale among his men by being in the thick of fighting and taking the trouble to know many personally
- moving quickly and effectively by dividing his forces and concentrating them for battle
- using artillery well and concentrating fire
- using the doctrine of the central position – holding the centre and attacking the enemy flank to envelop the opposing forces.

In over 60 actions the French took 150,000 prisoners and decisively defeated larger forces.

Bonaparte made sure that bulletins made the most of the victories and his own reputation and he became a hero in France.

The Egyptian campaign 1798

This was an ambitious plan to undermine Britain by blocking its overland trade routes to India and establishing a French presence in the Middle East by taking Egypt, then part of the Ottoman (Turkish) Empire. In May a French expedition took Malta and landed at Alexandria in Egypt. Modern artillery and the battle tactic of line and column in a mixed order led to a victory over Egyptian forces at the Battle of the Pyramids with few losses. However, on 1 August the British revealed a major limitation in Napoleon's strength by destroying the French fleet in Alexandria at the Battle of the Nile. The British ships, led by the great British naval commander Nelson, daringly raided the French by sailing in low water between the French ships and the shore. The French army, though victorious, was stranded. They advanced into Gaza and took Jaffa and Haifa. At Jaffa 1,400 prisoners were killed and the city plundered.

Napoleon left his army, which was now suffering from disease, and returned to France. His reputation was not diminished by the essential failure of this expedition, but rather was heightened with more evidence of his military triumphs.

Simple essay style

Below is a sample exam question. Use your own knowledge, information on the opposite page and information from other sections of the book to produce a plan for this question. Choose four general points, and provide three pieces of specific information to support each general point. Once you have planned your essay, write the introduction and conclusion for the essay. The introduction should list the points to be discussed in the essay and outline the line of argument you intend to take. The conclusion should summarise the key points and justify which point was the most important.

Assess the reasons for Napoleon's early military successes.

Turning assertion into argument

a

Below are a sample question and a series of assertions. Read the exam question and then add a justification to each of the assertions to turn each one into an argument.

'Napoleon's early military successes depended a lot on the weaknesses of his enemies.' How far do you agree?

Napoleon's own military abilities were the key reason for his early success as a general because …

However, in many instances, he faced weak enemies, as in Italy where …

Also, in Egypt, Napoleon did not face modern forces because …

The weaknesses of the Directory and the Coup of Brumaire

REVISED

The rise to power of Bonaparte was a result both of his own reputation and abilities and the weaknesses of the Directory.

The decline in power and popularity of the Directory

A number of events, decisions and developments in 1798 and 1799 contributed to this decline.

Jourdan's Law, September 1798

Conscription was reintroduced to rebuild the size of the army. This provoked widespread resistance.

The Second Coalition

Encouraged by British success, the Second Coalition of Britain, Austria, Russia, the Ottoman Empire, Naples and Portugal was formed in 1799. As the revolutionary war continued the French armies were pushed back into France from Germany and Italy. This meant the Directory could not continue to be funded by plunder. And the threat of invasion made it unpopular. There was increasing disillusion with the Directory and support for a change of government.

Coup of Prairial, June 1799

With the war going badly and the Directors getting the blame, the influence of the **neo-Jacobins** in the Councils increased. They forced the removal of two Directors and passed two new laws. The first was a forced loan on the rich.

The Coup of Brumaire

In late 1799 **Abbé Sieyès**, a leading revolutionary figure since 1789 and now a Director, plotted a coup. He wanted to restore the power of the executive and cut back the influence of the radicals. He needed the support of the army and of a general, and his eventual choice was Napoleon.

Sieyès moved the Councils out of Paris to Saint Cloud on 10 November 1799 on the pretext of a neo-Jacobin plot. Napoleon was persuaded to address the Councils. In the Council of Five Hundred Napoleon was attacked by deputies, but his soldiers, alerted by his brother, came to his rescue. The Councils were cleared from their meeting rooms by military force and the plotters issued a decree abolishing the Directory. Instead there was to be a government headed by three leaders, called consuls. However, Napoleon dominated. He was First Consul for ten years with complete executive power in war and peace. The other two consuls merely accepted his rule and became simply advisers. Napoleon was responsible for the new constitution of 1799.

The plotting within the Directory and the problems and dangers it faced had led to moves to strengthen the government to resist possible changes by either royalists or Jacobins and to deal more effectively with internal and external problems. The use of military force in the coup made it difficult to resist, but opponents were unlikely to gain popular support for resistance as Bonaparte was a famous and prestigious figure. The coup was not well managed in itself, but the combination of divisions within the Directory, pressing threats and problems and a popular new leader made it a success.

The new constitution

The male population (c.6,000,000) chose the Communal List (600,000), who chose the Department List (60,000), who chose the National List, the Notables (6,000).

The Notables

This was the key group. They were the highest-taxed men, the richest, in each department. They were to be replaced every three years. From their number the Senate, chosen by the executive, chose the members of the legislative bodies, who were to serve for five years:

Tribunate	Legislature
• 100 members aged over 25 • Discussed legislation drafted by the Senate but not able to vote on it	• 300 members aged over 30 • Voted on legislation in secret but not able to discuss it

The executive was made up of the First Consul and the Senate and Council of State, all chosen by the First Consul:

The First Consul	Senate	Council of State
• Appointed all ministers and initiated all legislation • Along with the other two consuls, was elected for ten years	• 60 members aged over 40 • Appointed for life • Nominated by the First Consul • Verified legislation	• 30–40 members chosen by the First Consul • Nominated all central and local officials • Helped initiate legislation

The new constitution was put to the people in a **plebiscite** (referendum) which was rigged to give an overwhelming majority in favour. In 1802 it was amended to make Napoleon Consul for Life.

Turning assertion into argument

Below are a sample question and a series of assertions. Read the exam question and then add a justification to each of the assertions to turn it into an argument.

To what extent did Napoleon gain power because of the weaknesses of the Directory?

Napoleon depended on the weaknesses of the Directory to gain power because ...

Napoleon had shown himself to be a brilliant and successful leader so he was a strong candidate to take power because ...

Napoleon achieved power only because of intrigues within the Directory because ...

Use own knowledge to support or contradict

a

Below is an interpretation about the rise of Napoleon Bonaparte. You are asked to summarise the interpretation, then use your own knowledge to agree and then to contradict.

'The regime was tottering. Royalist rebels controlled large areas of western France. France was verging on bankruptcy. The Directory was feeble and discredited. That autumn Paris looked to him, talked of him as the one man who could save the Republic. His rise to power depended on that sense of crisis.'

Adapted from: Corelli Barnett, *Bonaparte* (1978)

Summary:

Agree with the interpretation:

Contradict the interpretation:

Napoleon's reforms as Consul: political, administrative and legal changes

REVISED

Napoleon dominated the Consulate government and after 1801 could devote himself to reforms in France. Many of the changes were linked to his need to maintain a high level of personal power. However, there were many changes which carried on the work done by the Revolution and could be seen as significant reforms.

Political change

Napoleon brought about significant political changes.

Napoleon's consolidation of power

In February 1800 Napoleon changed how the 83 departments of France were administered. At their head were **prefects**. They had wide powers and responsibilities, including appointing those officials who served under them. As they were appointed and replaced by the First Consul they were agents of central government. The First Consul also appointed the mayors in major towns and nominated the members of the various councils that existed at department and municipal levels. So as First Consul Napoleon exercised highly centralised control of the administration of France as well as considerable powers of patronage.

Consul for Life

In December 1800 an assassination attempt on Napoleon failed. Although it was planned by royalists, Napoleon used it as the pretext to deal with neo-Jacobins too. A hundred neo-Jacobins were deported. The plot also highlighted how dependent the regime was on Napoleon and this led the Senate to offer Napoleon the Consulship for life. He accepted on the condition that the people agreed, and in the plebiscite referendum that followed over 3,500,000 voted yes with just over 8,000 against. As with each of the plebiscites held, there are debates about how accurate the figures are. Historians agree that there was vote-rigging and misreporting. Nevertheless, Napoleon became Consul for Life.

At the same time the Senate was enlarged and the Legislature had more of Napoleon's supporters appointed, giving him greater control of both. Meanwhile, the Tribunate was purged in 1802 for opposing the Civil Code.

Legal and administrative change

There were far-reaching legal and administrative changes.

The Civil Code, 21 March 1804

The legal system that emerged from the Revolution was reformed by the Civil Code. This was a clear statement of the law, and Napoleon was actively involved in the debates on its formulation in the Senate although he did not always get his own way. It can be viewed as having two strands, one liberal, confirming some of the changes of the Revolution, and one illiberal, confirming traditional authority.

- It introduced a common law code for the whole of France and was applicable to all citizens who were to have civil rights.
- Judges were to be guided by laws but when there were no relevant laws they were to use their own judgement.
- The legal rights of those who had bought land confiscated from the Church and nobility were upheld and could not be challenged.
- The system of inheritance – **partage** – introduced by the Revolution was changed. Property owners were allowed to bequeath their lands as they wished and the lands did not have to pass to the eldest son.
- Abolition of feudalism was confirmed.
- The privileges of the Catholic Church were removed.

These elements showed the influence of the Revolution, but other aspects were less liberal:

- The reintroduction of slavery in French colonies was permitted.
- Considerable authority was given to the male head of households. Women were expected to obey their husbands and children expected to obey their fathers. Unfaithful wives and disobedient children could be imprisoned.
- Married women could not own property independently of their husbands or administer common property independently.
- Divorce requirements were different for women than men – adultery was grounds for divorcing a wife but only if the other woman were actually brought into the home could it be grounds for women to divorce their husbands.
- Husbands had custody rights over children.

Support or challenge? a

Below is an exam-style question which asks you how far you agree with a specific statement. Below this is a series of general statements which are relevant to the question. Using your own knowledge and the information on the opposite page and page 54, decide which general statements support or challenge the statement in the question and tick the appropriate box.

'Napoleon's accession to power meant an authoritarian dictatorship.' How far do you agree?

	Support	Challenge
He set up prefects in the 83 departments.		
In 1802 Napoleon became Consul for Life.		
Napoleon held plebiscites on major issues.		
There was a new legal code for the whole of France.		
The abolition of feudalism was confirmed.		
The authority of fathers and husbands over women was strengthened.		
The Tribunate could discuss laws but not vote and the Senate could vote but not discuss laws.		
The male population could vote.		
The male population voted for a list of electors who in turn voted for another list of electors for the Tribunate.		

Delete as applicable a

Below are a sample exam question and a paragraph written in answer to this question. Read the paragraph and decide which of the options (in bold) is the most appropriate. Delete the least appropriate options and complete the paragraph by justifying your selection.

How significant was the Civil Code of 1804?

The codification of all laws into a single code was **a very important/a minor/an unpopular** development. It established that all citizens should have civil rights and equal justice so this showed that the work of the Revolution was **being continued/being ignored/being reversed.** The Code was **popular/unpopular/a matter of indifference** for property owners. The Code was **very liberal/partly liberal/completely illiberal.** The Code was **favourable/unfavourable/irrelevant** for the position of women. Divorce law made men and women **equal/unequal.** The Code reflected Napoleon's own ideas on authority and discipline **to a large extent/not at all/only in terms of women.**

Napoleon's reforms as Consul: social and economic changes

REVISED

In the Consulate there were important social and economic changes. Education reform was particularly significant and long-lasting.

Education

The purpose of education, according to Napoleon, was to provide France with administrators, officials and military officers. These would be recruited from the sons of the property-owning class, the Notables. Their sons were to be educated in one of the 45 *lycées* or elite schools established in 1802. Places were free for the sons of army officers. Additionally about 300 secondary schools were established in the years after 1805. In all a common curriculum was taught by government-appointed teachers using the same textbooks and standardised lessons. This system was eventually controlled by the Imperial University, established in 1808. The second purpose of education was to bind the state together through standardisation; achieved by creating a body of teachers with a common purpose who would produce a generation with the same outlook and attitudes.

Those who wanted a more questioning education for their children sent them to the more expensive private schools run by the Church, which were allowed after the Concordat.

At the primary level schools were run by individuals, by the Church and by local communities. They provided moral education and basic literacy and numeracy, which was all ordinary people were thought to need. Scientific study and enquiry for its own sake were not encouraged and the higher education establishment the École Polytechnique, established earlier in the Revolution, was converted into a military academy in 1805. However, the main university of France, the Sorbonne in Paris, and provincial universities were reopened.

The position of the Church

Napoleon recognised the need to resolve the crucial conflict between the Catholic Church and the state.

The Concordat and its aftermath

Negotiations with the papacy began in 1800 and culminated in the Concordat, which was signed in 1801. Under its terms:

- The Catholic Church recognised the Revolution and agreed not try to regain its lands.
- The Church was to be state controlled with its clergy appointed and paid by the government to which they had to swear loyalty.
- Toleration of other faiths including Jews was to be allowed.

To this agreement Napoleon added the 'Organic Articles', which limited papal control over French bishops while increasing the French government's control over priests.

With the Concordat Napoleon secured a tax-paying Church obedient to the state. The threat of royalism was reduced. In 1806, despite papal objections, he even felt able to amend the church **catechisms** to teach the people to revere and obey Napoleon himself. He went so far as to create a new St Napoleon's Day on 16 August.

Financial reforms

Centralised control led to great improvements. The main direct tax was the land tax. Land registers showing ownership were drawn up and the tax registers showing who should pay were improved. These steps made tax collection fair and efficient.

The Bank of France

This was founded by Napoleon in 1800 as a private bank but had a range of public functions including the sole right to issue paper notes. It later had strict controls placed upon its actions. Having a central bank made the government's task of raising finance much easier, something the Ancien Régime crucially lacked.

The currency

Napoleon introduced a new currency, the *franc de germinal*, based upon gold and silver coins. Strict control of the metal content ensured that this was a stable currency which provided a strong base for the French economy, something that the revolutionary paper-based *assignat* had failed to do.

Support or challenge?

Below is an exam-style question which asks you how far you agree with a specific statement. Below this is a series of general statements which are relevant to the question. Using your own knowledge and the information on the opposite page and page 56, decide which general statements support or challenge the statement in the question and tick the appropriate box.

'The reforms of the Consulate were simply a way of increasing the power of Napoleon.' How far do you agree?

	Support	Challenge
Toleration of other faiths was confirmed by the Concordat.		
The loss of Church lands was confirmed and their new owners safeguarded.		
New catechisms were introduced so that the Church urged people to obey Napoleon.		
16 August was made St Napoleon's Day.		
New secondary schools were set up.		
The government appointed teachers and set down the curriculum.		
Education aimed to provide France with officials and well-educated officers.		
The currency was stabilised.		
There were new registers drawn up for the land tax.		

Developing an argument

a

Below are a sample exam question, a list of key points to be made in the essay, and a paragraph from the essay. Read the question, the key points and the sample paragraph. Using the information from the opposite page and from page 56, rewrite the paragraph in order to develop an argument. Your paragraph should try to balance the benefits against the disadvantages.

How far did the reforms of the Consulate benefit the people of France?

Key points:

- Reassured Catholics
- Improved state finances
- Helped property owners
- Educational changes
- Religious toleration
- Much to do with reinforcing Napoleon's authority.

Sample paragraph:

Many of the reforms of the Consulate were beneficial. After the revolutionary years there was more stability and Napoleon introduced some changes, like legal reforms, which had begun in the revolutionary years but had not been completed. Educational reforms were beneficial for some, with more schools and universities and more study of applied scientific and technical subjects. The Church reforms helped a lot of French people to be loyal to France without feeling they were betraying their religion and also extended toleration. A sign of stability was the new currency backed by a new Bank of France. However, not all of the reforms were aimed to benefit the people and some were more concerned with Napoleon's power and authority.

Napoleon's military successes and failures after 1799

The army and conquest during the Consulate and Empire

Napoleon needed a military success to consolidate his Consulship. He crossed the Alps and defeated the Austrians at Marengo in June 1800. Napoleon claimed this as his victory but much was owed to his subordinate Desaix, who used his own initiative to return to the battlefield to save Napoleon from attack at the cost of his own life. Victory enhanced Bonaparte's popularity but the Austrians were only willing to negotiate peace after General Moreau's victory at Hohenlinden in Bavaria, December 1800. With the Second Coalition destroyed (see page 54), Britain was also prepared to negotiate. The Peace of Amiens was agreed in March 1802, but did not last. In the interim Napoleon failed to recapture the Caribbean colony of Saint-Domingue and sold Louisiana to the United States.

The War of the Third Coalition, 1805–06

The Napoleonic Wars broke out again in May 1803 and the Third Coalition had formed by 1805. The Russian Tsar was angry at the shooting of the Duc d'Enghien (see page 62) and French actions in Germany, while the Austrians were angered by French expansion in Italy. Napoleon's plans for invading Britain were finally destroyed by defeat at the **Battle of Trafalgar**, October, 1805. In the following three months he won a swift series of victories over the Austrians at Ulm in October and over the Austrians and Russians at Austerlitz in December. The Russians retreated while Austria agreed a separate peace giving France control of Northern Italy.

This war was the high point of Napoleon's military success and showed the key elements of his skills as a commander at their most developed. The rapid march from Boulogne to Ulm in 1805 took his Austrian enemies by surprise and defeated them before they could be joined by their Russian allies. He divided his forces, lived off the land and assembled them quickly and effectively to outmanoeuvre the Austrians and to gain a victory without a large-scale engagement. He had the confidence and courage to plunge deep into Europe mid-winter and to take every advantage of the weaknesses of his Russian enemies at the battle of Austerlitz. He dared to maintain a weak and seemingly vulnerable right flank which lured the Russians into an attack, exposing their centre. A classic enveloping manoeuvre left Napoleon commanding the heights at the centre and being able to cut off the Russians, inflicting heavy casualties as they attempted to retreat. Much depended on his inspiring his troops to hold the deliberately weakened right flank.

The War of the Fourth Coalition, 1806–07

War with Prussia was provoked by Napoleon's attempts to impose his Continental System (see page 68) and expanding influence in Germany. Prussia was decisively defeated in the Battles of Jena and Auerstädt, October 1806. Here there was less assurance shown. Only the bravery and determination of Napoleon's subordinate Davout saved the day at Jena when Napoleon divided his forces unwisely and left his smaller force to deal with the bulk of the Prussian army. Thereafter Napoleon advanced through Poland to attack Russia in 1807 and – after a hard fight – won the Battles of Eylau in February and Friedland in June. Napoleon was able to force Russia and Prussia to negotiate the Treaty of Tilsit, July 1807. This essentially divided Europe between the French and Russian Empires.

Napoleon's failure at sea

Napoleon had survived the consequences of error at Marengo (1800) and in the war against Prussia (1806) but his greatest failure was the defeat at Trafalgar which confirmed Britain's naval dominance. This led Napoleon into an economic war against Britain which had severe consequences (see page 68) and also meant that Britain persisted in its opposition, supporting coalitions against Napoleon which finally defeated him in 1814.

Reasons for military success by 1807

The part played by Napoleon

Napoleon was an able general. He:

- inspired personal devotion from his troops, utilising such devices as his bulletins and orders to his troops
- organised the French armies to combine flexibility with central command, e.g. corps of 25,000 to 30,000 men
- utilised new aggressive tactics such as making units on the march independent so they could live off the land and move quickly
- controlled every detail
- made good decisions on the battlefield, for example at Austerlitz.

The weaknesses of his enemies

- The superior combined forces of the coalitions were continually hampered by their failure to co-ordinate. Often they pursued their separate aims.
- Their armies lacked good artillery and their tactics were old-fashioned and static.

The strength of the Grande Armée

This was created by Napoleon between 1801 and 1805, building upon the mass conscript armies of the Revolution. Its size, morale, organisation and enthusiasm were superior to those of any of the enemies it faced and its officers were better as a result of promotion by merit.

Recommended reading

As the extent of Napoleon's genius as a commander is an area of great historical debate and is part of the topics that could be set for the AS interpretation question, it is worth spending some time studying it in some depth as it will enhance your understanding of the debate. Below is a list of suggested further reading on this topic:

- Corelli Barnett, *Bonaparte*, pages 92–129, Allen and Unwin (1978)
- David Gates, *The Napoleonic Wars*, Pimlico (2000)
- Andrew Roberts, *Napoleon the Great*, pages 357–463, Allen Lane (2014)
- Andrina Styles and Dylan Rees, *Access to History: Napoleon, France and Europe*, pages 77-83, Hodder (2004)
- D.G. Wright, *Longman Seminar Studies in History: Napoleon and Europe*, pages 45–48 (1984)

Use own knowledge to support or contradict

a

Below is an interpretation about Napoleon as commander. You are asked to summarise the interpretation, then use your own knowledge to agree and then to contradict.

> 'Napoleon recognised that modern wars – his wars – would be won by lightning strokes against the main enemy. His understanding of topography and mathematics allowed him to use artillery to maximum effect. He was able to keep the initiative in campaigns whose success were mainly a result of his inspired leadership. He was a genuine military genius.'
>
> Adapted from: Andrew Roberts, *Napoleon the Great* (2014)

Summary:

Agree with the interpretation:

Contradict the interpretation:

The establishment and nature of the Empire

REVISED

In 1804 a plot was uncovered to murder Napoleon and replace him with the Duc d'Enghien, a member of the Bourbon royal family, who was waiting just over the border in Baden. D'Enghien was kidnapped, tried for conspiracy and shot in what some saw as a judicial murder. The property-owning classes feared the reintroduction of the monarchy with its threat of returning all land to its original owners and so supported the formal proposal of the Senate that Napoleon be made hereditary Emperor of France. A third plebiscite confirmed that the people agreed. Although the turnout was lower than in previous plebiscites, this still showed that Napoleon had support. On 2 December 1804 Napoleon crowned himself Emperor in Paris in the presence of the Pope and then crowned his wife Joséphine as Empress.

Constitutional developments

Following Napoleon's coronation the Tribunate and Legislature were rarely consulted. The latter was formally abolished in 1808 while the former survived only by not challenging Napoleon's wishes. Government was conducted through the Senate and the Council of State, both firmly under Napoleon's control.

Class distinctions and titles

During his reign Napoleon worked to create a body of men who were loyal to him, especially soldiers. He was also effective in winning over many politicians who had initially opposed Brumaire. He did this through gifts, honours, titles and lands.

1 The Legion of Honour was created in 1802. Recipients received a medal which it was fashionable to wear plus an annual sum, quite small for most, but higher for the highest ranks of the order. There were 38,000 members, mostly soldiers, by 1814.
2 Between 1804 and 1808 new titles were created for the leading officials of the new imperial court. Again there were differing ranks. Some came with lands. Initially these were given to members of Napoleon's family but later to his leading generals, the marshals of France. After 1808 an entire imperial nobility was created with princes, dukes, counts and barons. If the recipients of these new honours had a large enough income their title could be made hereditary.
3 Members of the Senate were given large country estates with an annual income and appointed as prefects in their region.
4 At the lower end of the social scale more minor army officers and government officials were given personal gifts such as enough money to buy a house in Paris and live comfortably.

Establishment of Emperor status

Napoleon moved into the Tuileries Palace and began to develop a court life with ceremonies and etiquette. *Émigrés* were allowed to return. Napoleon was depicted as the heir to the great medieval emperor Charlemagne and adopted the bee as a royal symbol.

Censorship and propaganda

Napoleon's regime wanted to control what was published in France. In January 1800, 60 Parisian newspapers were closed. By the end of the year, four more had been shut down, leaving just nine. By 1811 there were only four, each with its own censor. Editors were expected to avoid controversial subjects and to rely for their news on the official government publications, especially its journal *Le Moniteur*. Provincial newspapers were subjected to similar censorship and control.

All other publications – books, plays, lectures and posters – were reported on and censored. By 1810 there was a formal system of censors. There was a secret police and networks of informers. Napoleon relied on a more developed system of surveillance and control than was usual in the Europe of his time.

Cult of Napoleon

At the same time Napoleon utilised the propaganda value of the visual arts. As well as buildings and the 'Empire' style, he utilised painters, notably the French artist Jacques-Louis David, to depict him in carefully controlled heroic style. For example, the iconic painting *Napoleon Crossing the Alps* depicts Napoleon on a prancing stallion, whereas, in reality, he crossed the Alps riding a mule.

Simple essay style

Below is a sample exam question. Use your own knowledge, information on the opposite page and information from other sections of the book to produce a plan for this question. Choose four general points, and provide three pieces of specific information to support each general point. Once you have planned your essay, write the introduction and conclusion for the essay. The introduction should list the points to be discussed in the essay and outline the line of argument you intend to take. The conclusion should summarise the key points and justify which point was the most important.

'The creation of the Empire in 1804 shows that Napoleon had betrayed the Revolution.' How far do you agree?

Turning assertion into argument

Below are a sample question and a series of assertions. Read the exam question and then add a justification to each of the assertions to turn each one into an argument.

'A corrupt police state.' How far do you agree with this view of the Empire in France 1804–14?

It could be argued that the Napoleonic Empire was corrupt because ...

The Empire had many characteristic of a police state because ...

However, by modern standards it did not have that much control of its people because ...

Exam focus

REVISED

Below are a sample exam question and a model answer. Read the question and then the answer and the comments around it.

How far were Napoleon's military successes before 1807 the result of his own military abilities?

Napoleon's own abilities were of great importance to his victories. He absorbed a lot from the military theorists of the eighteenth century and was able to use this effectively. It was his speed of movement, his eye for the battlefield, his use of artillery and his ability to motivate his men that were of considerable importance. However, this does not explain the extent of his victories and his own bulletins overestimated his influence. He inherited a large and well-motivated army and his opponents showed considerable weakness. Without this he would not have been able to win such decisive victories as those of 1805. There are also times when his leadership was not decisive. Thus an explanation which only dealt with Napoleon's military abilities would be a one-sided view of the reasons for his successes and cannot be accepted.

> The first part deals squarely with the key idea in the question and gives confidence that the candidate is responding to it.

> The introduction deftly introduces a counter-view.

> The view is offered that Napoleon's abilities cannot completely explain his victories – though this could be a bit more confident.

One of the key elements which Napoleon brought to his campaigns was the ability to motivate his troops. In 1796 he was especially successful in leading a force which had not achieved much victory into a spectacular campaign in Italy. He could not rely on his experience of leadership but had to motivate his men by example, his knowledge of artillery, his personal bravery and his confidence in victory. This set the tone for much of his campaigning. He created a legend of 'the little corporal'; his orders contained inspiring words; he took the trouble to get to know his men and he motivated his commanders. His manoeuvres depended on his troops having the confidence to hold their positions as at Austerlitz. However, he was not motivating inexperienced troops or raw recruits. He inherited strong revolutionary forces and even the Army of Italy was experienced. He also abandoned his forces in Egypt in 1798, showing that he put his own ambitions before their welfare.

> The first paragraph identifies a key attribute.

> There is some explanation and one precise example.

> There is some balance – but it would have helped to have had an interim judgement.

Even if his troops were well motivated, his victories depended to an extent on his enemies being slower and less mobile than his own forces. The Austrian forces in Italy in 1796–97 were taken aback by his rapid manoeuvres and at Ulm in 1805 the Austrians had failed to meet up with the Russian troops and allowed themselves to be surrounded. This showed considerable military weakness and, though Napoleon was able to take advantage of it, this helped him to victory.

> A counter-argument is now considered and explained.

> There is a touch of discussion here but again a more developed interim judgement would have helped.

The greatest example of the mixture of incompetent enemies and skilful leadership by Napoleon can be seen at Austerlitz in December 1805. Napoleon did arrive at the battlefield rapidly but his trick of leaving his right flank seemingly exposed to lure the Russians into a trap depended on military incompetence by his enemies. It allowed Napoleon to occupy the central position and sweep round the back of his enemies. However, this might well have failed had he been facing a better opponent.

> There is some detail here which develops the interrelationship between enemy weakness and Napoleon's own skills.

Also, though Napoleon won great victories before 1807, there were times when he faced defeat and was saved only by the skill of his subordinates. The most obvious example is at the Battle of Marengo in 1800 when he thought he had been victorious and sent Desaix away from the battlefield only to find he had been mistaken. Desaix returned to save Napoleon at the expense of his own life. A second example was in the campaign against Prussia in 1806 when Napoleon split his forces only to leave Davout facing the larger Prussian army with a smaller force while he faced a smaller Prussian army with the bulk of his own. It could be argued that Napoleon's genius meant that his commanders were inspired to fight as Napoleon himself would have fought, but it is more realistic to see mistakes being saved by brave subordinates.

Napoleon's military understanding was strong on land. He knew about infantry and made this an effective part of his battles from the siege of Toulon onwards. He had an eye for the battlefield and drew up his forces in a very effective way as at the Battle of the Pyramids, again against a weaker enemy with less advanced equipment and tactics. However, he had less success with naval strategy and the defeat at Trafalgar showed the weakness of French naval power.

It is probably fair to say that his greatest ability was to take advantage of favourable circumstances. He saw quickly when his enemies were divided and moved to defeat them quickly before they could unite. He took advantage of previous reformers' ideas, for example, when organising his troops into self-sufficient corps, dividing on the way to battle and uniting for the actual conflict. He also saw, in the light of the enthusiasm of the revolutionary armies, how important image and morale were, unlike his enemies, who often relied on brutal discipline and aristocratic commanders who expected obedience. However, this did mean that Napoleon could not be seen entirely as responsible for his own victories. He depended too heavily on earlier reforms, on the Revolution and on weak enemies for his success to be as attributable to his own genius as he made out.

The idea that Napoleon was dependent on others is introduced.

There is good support here.

There is a discussion here which might have been a bit more developed but there is more than just a list of factors.

The point about the sea rather hangs in the air and is not developed.

This is a well-balanced, analytical paragraph and there is a view offered.

The answer would reach the higher levels, but not the very top. Some of the interim judgements could be developed and in places some of the analysis is a bit slim compared to the knowledge imparted. The impact of sea power might be explored further.

Reaching the top level

Use the comments and the mark scheme to move the response to the very top level, making a list of the additional features that would enable the answer to achieve full marks. Remember it does not have to be a perfect answer, only one that is a better fit with the descriptors.

Exam focus

REVISED

Below are a sample exam question for the AS-level interpretation question and a model answer. Read the question and then the answer and the comments around it.

'The Directory was unpopular and could not meet the needs of the French middle classes who were threatened by war, religious divisions and political extremism. The plotters needed a popular general but at first Bonaparte was not on the short list. The Directory was already weak and little pressure was needed to send it toppling.'

From: Martyn Lyons, *Napoleon Bonaparte and the Legacy of the French Revolution* (1994)

Evaluate the strengths and limitations of this interpretation, making reference to other interpretations that you have studied.

The interpretation puts forward the view that Napoleon came to power largely because of the weakness and unpopularity of the Directory, who could not solve military problems or deal with the divide between Catholic opponents of the Revolution and the revolutionary regime that emerged in 1795. There was also the issue of political extremism, with a civil war in some provinces and, in Paris, both royalist and Jacobin opponents of the Directory. It argues that the weak government was on the point of collapse and it was not necessarily the popularity and prestige of Napoleon that brought about the fall, which is an alternative explanation, but its own internal weaknesses.

> The interpretation is clearly explained and this allows the response to identify key areas that can be examined for strengths and limitations.

> The interpretation is placed in the wider context of the debate about the Coup of Brumaire.

In some ways this is justified and shows that the interpretation has strengths. In support of the interpretation given here that the key element was the weakness of the Directory rather than Napoleon's influence, which does offer a convincing analysis of some of the problems by 1799, it is true that the Directory had severe weaknesses. When the regime was threatened by a royalist uprising at Vendémiaire in October 1795 it was the army led by Napoleon and his use of cannon that saved the day. And again later when the Directors were threatened by the election of so many neo-Jacobin deputies it was the army that they relied upon to enforce their actions. There were economic and financial weaknesses, too, and this suggests that the interpretation is accurate. In February 1797 the paper currency, the *assignat*, had to be withdrawn because it had plummeted in value. The Directors' efforts to reform the paper currency failed and in 1787 metal coins were the only currency; as there was a shortage of coinage this hampered economic activity. The fall in value of government bonds, which became known as the bankruptcy of two-thirds, reduced confidence in the regime. The government had to rely on violence more and more. This suggests a strength of the interpretation. The Coup of Prairial shows they were reliant on force.

> The answer makes it clear what it is going to do – to support the view in the passage.

> A strength of the interpretation is identified and own knowledge is used directly to confirm it, organising the points well.

The Directory had managed to stay in power but only at the price of undermining its own democratic foundation. This marked the start of its failure.

> A second area of strength is explained by using own knowledge about the problem of political violence and unrest.

The Directors were divided among themselves and plotted the end of the 1795 constitution, hoping to use military power. Thus it could be argued that the Directory was so weak that any successful general would have served to overthrow it.

> The response considers a range of issues raised by the interpretation. It sums up clearly.

However, this interpretation is not entirely convincing and has limitations. It was not merely the weaknesses of the Directory but Napoleon's considerable popularity and prestige that brought him to power. It was not merely that he was a successful general, but that he was particularly outstanding and had caught the imagination of France. Napoleon's victories in Italy had done much to strengthen the Directory. The benefits of this were the plunder and payments extorted from the defeated enemies, the new territories of Nice and Savoy that were annexed and the creation of satellites – the Cisalpine and Ligurian Republics. These were a source of income and men for France's armies. Also Napoleon had become very famous and very popular. This is something that the interpretation does not stress enough and so it can seen as having limitations. Since his early victory over the British at Toulon Napoleon had been well known. His own bulletins spread his fame, his exploits in Egypt had made him a hero and by setting up new states in Italy, and for a while in Egypt, and by negotiating with Austria, he appeared as a statesman, more than just a general. The coup needed someone the army would support and also someone who was a natural leader. To suggest that it was just the weaknesses of the Directory may be misleading and also underestimates some of the achievements of the regime, such as its financial reforms and its ability to suppress opposition. Despite the weaknesses of the Directory, its overthrow depended heavily on the special prestige and popularity of Napoleon, who was quick to take personal power and end any reliance on the plotters. This means that the interpretation has limitations as well as strengths as this aspect is not sufficiently considered. It must be seen that Napoleon was the key to the Coup of Brumaire.

The counter-view is introduced clearly.

There is supported evidence that the Directory was not completely weak.

Napoleon's strengths are explained. The answer does not go into descriptions, but makes the point about popularity and political experience.

Further evidence for limitations to the interpretation are given and directly linked back to it.

The answer offers a view.

The response is able to place the interpretation in the wider context of the debate about Brumaire and does not get sidetracked by long accounts of Napoleon's campaigns, which are not needed to reach any level. The strengths and weaknesses of the interpretation are considered and the supporting knowledge is detailed and accurate. The interpretation is evaluated and there are clear examples of linking own knowledge to the actual interpretation to do this. As a result the response would reach the highest level.

Evaluating the interpretation

The key to a good answer is to evaluate the given interpretation and use your own knowledge to show the strengths and limitations of the interpretation. Go through the response and identify all the evaluative words that are used in the answer.

4 The decline and fall of Napoleon, 1807–15

The Continental System

REVISED

France was at war from 1803 to 1814 but the one opponent Napoleon Bonaparte was unable to defeat was Britain, protected as it was by its control of the seas secured after the Battle of Trafalgar in 1805. Thereafter the British fleet was able to blockade French ports. This led to a decline in the seaport economy linked to cities such as Bordeaux and Nantes.

The Continental System was designed by Napoleon as an economic attack on Britain. It was announced in the Berlin Decrees, November 1806, and extended in 1807 by the Milan Decrees. The decrees forbade any trade with Britain by France and the other satellite states in Napoleon's Empire. Napoleon hoped that by stopping British exports to the continent its economy and industries would be damaged. At the same time, allowing Britain to continue to import goods, but only with cash payment, would deplete the British economy still further, thus rendering Britain unable to continue the war. This would have the added benefit of protecting French industries from British competition both in France and in selling to the rest of the Empire.

Effects on France

The decline in the seaport economy included not just trade but also related industries such as ship-building and rope-making. Other French industries that relied upon export markets also suffered. However, in central and eastern France, trade routes along the Rhine and across the Alps opened new markets both in the Empire and bordering territories.

Effects on Britain

To begin with, the lack of French sea power hampered the effectiveness of the System. In 1809, in a twin-pronged policy, Napoleon improved efforts to seize and destroy smuggled goods and at the same time started to license some trade in grain and wine with Britain. Historians differ on how badly Britain was affected. Some argue Britain was affected very little, with new markets developing in North and South America, while others suggest that in 1811 Britain's trade with the continent fell by as much as 50 per cent. Undoubtedly Britain's efforts to counter-blockade France was one cause of the **Anglo-American War of 1812**.

Effects on Europe

The Continental System created tensions between Napoleon and some of the states within his Empire as well as those outside. For example, Portugal's refusal to take part led to the **Peninsular War** (see page 72) beginning in 1808, while Russia's withdrawal precipitated Napoleon's invasion of 1812.

Effects on Napoleon's downfall

The Continental System contributed to Napoleon's downfall in several ways:

- It failed to bring about British defeat.
- The need to enforce it by invading Portugal was a major element in involving France in the Peninsular War (see page 72), which drained resources and forced Napoleon into fighting on two fronts in 1812–14.
- The Russian campaign in 1812, which was a major factor in Napoleon's downfall, was partly a result of the Tsar's unwillingness to co-operate in the Continental System.
- Along with concerns about the human and financial costs of war, the economic problems in France contributed to unpopularity at home.

Mind map

Make a copy of the mind map below and use the information on the opposite page to add detail to it.

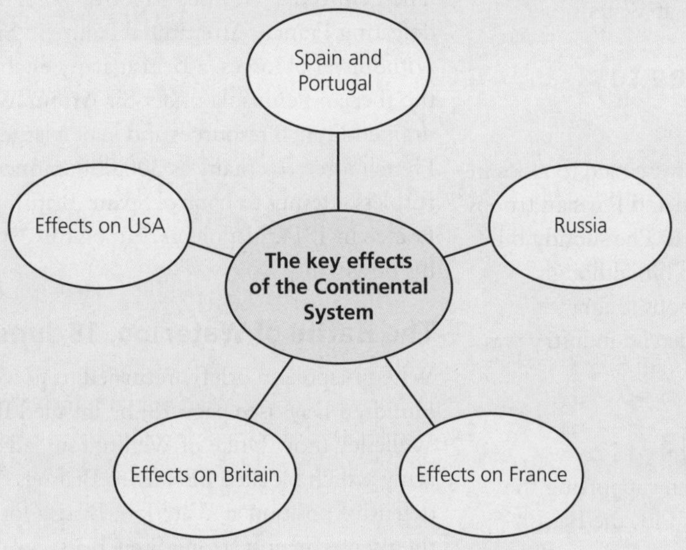

Develop the detail

a

Below are a question and a paragraph written in answer to this question. The paragraph contains a limited amount of detail. Annotate the paragraph to add additional detail to the answer.

Assess the importance of the Continental System for Napoleon's decline.

Napoleon hoped to use economic warfare and his predominance in Europe to defeat Britain so its failure was very significant for him. It meant that he had to face continuing hostility from Britain. The Continental System never achieved its aims but it had unintended consequences. This was true not only for France but for other European countries and it led Napoleon to force his control over a wider area. This in turn was a major cause of his downfall. It was typical of Napoleon's belief that his own willpower could achieve anything and was overambitious, with very severe consequences for him and his Empire.

The role of Britain in bringing about Napoleon's downfall

REVISED

Britain maintained constant opposition to Napoleon from 1803–14 and a British army in alliance with Prussia was responsible for his final defeat in 1815 at Waterloo.

British financial subsidies to Napoleon's enemies

Large subsidies (£600 million in all) were paid to allies in Europe and possibly 450,000 Austrian and Russian troops were being paid for by Britain by 1813. The subsidy bill reached £10 million a year by 1814. Thus although relatively small numbers of British troops fought Napoleon, the wealth of Britain's trade and industry was used against him.

British diplomatic efforts

British diplomacy played a large part in supporting the different coalitions against Napoleon. Pitt, the British prime minister, played a major part in organising the Third Coalition when the brief truce of 1802–03 broke down and Britain urged Europe to oppose Napoleon. British diplomacy helped to persuade Austria to oppose Napoleon in 1809 though it was defeated. It was particularly important in 1812 when Britain kept Austria, Prussia and Russia together in the final struggle.

British naval power

Britain kept up constant pressure against French trade and French imports of war supplies from neutral countries by its naval blockade against France. The Orders in Council gave Britain the legal right to stop and search any ship bound for a French port and seize its cargo. This led to an attack on Copenhagen in 1807 when Denmark seemed likely to join France in protest about this, and also led to a war against the USA in 1812. However, the blockade was damaging to France. British ships also acted against French privateers raiding British shipping.

There were also important naval victories, particularly the Battle of Trafalgar in October 1805, when the joint French and Spanish fleet was attacked and seriously weakened by Nelson's fleet, preventing any attempt to support an invasion of Britain. After this, Britain achieved naval domination. This protected the Channel and inflicted damage on French trade and colonies.

British land forces

The Peninsular War (see page 72) was a major element in defeating France. After initial failure in Spain and withdrawal of forces, a British army established itself in the Iberian Peninsula under Sir Arthur Wellesley. This drained French resources and kept a large number of French forces, as many as 300,000, pinned down in a ruthless attempt to control Spain. British forces invaded France in 1814. Napoleon blamed this 'Spanish ulcer' for his downfall.

The Battle of Waterloo, 18 June 1814

When Napoleon briefly returned to power in the Hundred Days (see page 78) he invaded Belgium. Wellesley (now Duke of Wellington) led an Anglo-Dutch army which blocked his way to Brussels. Taking a defensive position at Waterloo, British forces defended themselves against strong French attacks until the arrival of Prussian forces. The losses Napoleon suffered and his defeat ended the Hundred Days and he was taken captive and imprisoned on the British Atlantic island of St Helena where he died in 1821.

The British war effort

The long struggle against Napoleon was supported by a whole range of British workers, soldiers and sailors. British forces depended on the industrial growth of the British economy and its naval power on a whole support network of craftsmen, suppliers, farmers, merchant seamen and volunteers.

How important was the British war effort in defeating Napoleon?

- The 60,000 British troops did not match the hundreds of thousands fighting for and against France.
- Had Napoleon not been so intent on continuing the wars, then British diplomacy could not have rallied forces against him. His decision not to compromise after the defeat in 1812 played into British hands.
- The Continental System played a part in leading Napoleon into war in Russia in 1812, but was not the only reason.
- British naval power prevented an invasion but by itself could not bring about the defeat of Napoleon.

Support or challenge?

Below is an exam-style question which asks you how far you agree with a specific statement. Below this is a series of general statements which are relevant to the question. Using your own knowledge and the information on the opposite page and page 68, decide which general statements support or challenge the statement in the question and tick the appropriate box.

'Britain played the vital role in the defeat of Napoleon.' How far do you agree?

	Support	Challenge
60,000 British troops fought Napoleon.		
British naval power prevented Napoleon from invading Britain.		
To defeat Britain, Napoleon introduced the Continental System, which led him to overextend himself in Spain and Russia.		
The British navy blockaded France.		
The Continental System caused some hardship in Britain.		
In 1812 Britain went to war with the USA.		
The Battle of Waterloo depended on the arrival of Prussian troops.		
Britain financed European coalitions against Napoleon.		

Eliminate irrelevance

a

Below are a sample exam question and a paragraph written in answer to this question. Read the paragraph and, using the information from the opposite page, identify parts of the paragraph that are not directly relevant to the question. Draw a line through the information that is irrelevant and justify your deletions in the margin.

How important was Britain's control of the seas in the struggle against Napoleon?

Napoleon never saw the importance of sea power and suffered as a result. His genius was in land warfare and here rapid movement and concentration of force was the key. He attempted this at Trafalgar but the joint Franco-Spanish fleets were defeated by Nelson. Napoleon could not invade Britain but he had already given up this idea and marched his invasion force from Boulogne to the Danube where he defeated Austria. Britain's coalitions could not withstand Napoleon's forces. However, the supremacy of the navy allowed them to control the seas and blockade France, hitting French trade and war supplies. It also meant that Britain could supply and reinforce its forces in the key war in Portugal and Spain which drained so many French resources. This war had begun as a result of Napoleon's desire for even more European expansion. The Spanish resisted and Napoleon was drawn into a long conflict – the 'Spanish ulcer'. This did not deter him from embarking on another war against Austria in 1809.

The campaigns in Spain and Russia

REVISED

The Peninsular War, 1808–14

In May 1808, in an attempt to enforce the blockade in Spain, Napoleon replaced the Spanish king with his brother, Joseph. This was not a success. The Spanish did not welcome the French but rose in a revolt in Madrid that was brutally suppressed. This led to the outbreak of guerrilla warfare, which became a major factor in France's ultimate defeat. Meanwhile, a small French army was defeated by regular Spanish troops. News of this victory spread across Europe and in response Napoleon took his Grande Armée to Spain. Before he had time to fully complete its pacification he had to turn his attention to the Austrians. He never returned to Spain but the war there dragged on until 1814.

The French faced guerrilla warfare from the Spanish which tied down thousands of troops in garrisons and disrupted their lines of supply and communications. Plus they faced regular warfare from the British armies, under Wellesley, sent to aid their Portuguese ally in 1808. French efforts to drive the British out of Portugal in 1810–11 failed and when the war began to turn against Napoleon across Europe, Wellesley was able to move on to the attack. After a series of victories at Salamanca, 1812, and Vitoria, 1813, Spain was liberated and the French driven back over the Pyrenees.

While not a decisive theatre of the war, this conflict was a constant drain on French resources in terms of men, money, morale and prestige. Napoleon called it the 'Spanish ulcer'.

The Russian campaign, 1812

Tsar Alexander withdrew from the Continental System at the end of 1810. There were other sources of friction between the Russian Tsar and French Emperor:

- Napoleon's marriage to the Austrian princess, Marie Louise, in 1809, after divorcing the Empress Joséphine, since Russia and Austria were rivals.
- Rival ambitions to seize Turkish territory, including Istanbul, in the Balkans.
- Rival ambitions in the Baltic – Napoleon annexed the Duchy of Oldenburg; Alexander annexed Swedish Finland.
- Disagreement over the future of the Grand Duchy of Poland.

Napoleon assembled a huge army – 600,000 men. Fewer than half were French; the rest were drawn from throughout his Empire and from his allies. There were Austrians, Danes, Germans, Italians, Lithuanians, Prussians, Poles, Portuguese, Spanish and Swiss.

In June 1812 Napoleon invaded Russia. Despite his victory at Borodino in September and the subsequent occupation of Moscow, the Tsar refused to negotiate a peace treaty, and Napoleon was forced to retreat. The campaign was a disaster for a number of reasons:

- The Russians, apart from at Borodino, refused to fight the formal battle that Napoleon believed would give him a decisive victory.
- The Russians adopted a scorched earth strategy, destroying all food and supplies on Napoleon's line of march and so preventing his army from living off the land as it usually did.
- Russian skirmishers constantly attacked, killing many and damaging morale.
- The Russian army was much larger.
- Napoleon lacked a clear strategic objective.
- His approach of controlling every detail could not work with such large armies across such vast territory.
- Poor supply and medical arrangements meant thousands of his men died or were incapacitated by disease.
- He stayed in Moscow for over a month before recognising the need to retreat.

When the Grande Armée reached Germany again it was reduced to approximately 120,000 men. Napoleon left it to return swiftly to France to restore his position there. He later blamed his defeat on the Russian winter, but historians point to the high casualties his army suffered even before the worst winter weather began.

Simple essay style

Below is a sample exam question. Use your own knowledge, information on the opposite page and information from other sections of the book to produce a plan for this question. Choose four general points, and provide three pieces of specific information to support each general point. Once you have planned your essay, write the introduction and conclusion for the essay. The introduction should list the points to be discussed in the essay and outline the line of argument you intend to take. The conclusion should summarise the key points and justify which point was the most important.

Assess the importance of the Russian campaign in 1812 for the defeat of Napoleon.

Turning assertion into argument

a

Below are a sample question and a series of assertions. Read the exam question and then add a justification to each of the assertions to turn each one into an argument.

'The campaign in Russia in 1812 was the main reason for Napoleon's downfall.' How far do you agree?

The defeat in Russia meant that Napoleon was put on the road to eventual ruin because ...

However, the war in Spain was seen by Napoleon himself as more important because ...

Yet it was not as important because ...

The campaigns of 1813–14 and Napoleon's abdication

REVISED

The War of the Sixth Coalition, 1813–14

Following the Russian disaster, the Sixth Coalition against Napoleon formed. This comprised Britain and Russia and his recent, reluctant allies, initially Prussia and then also Austria. What set this coalition apart from its predecessors were five factors:

1. It had a common aim, the liberation of Germany.
2. It included all four major European powers.
3. Its members had reformed their armies and tactics.
4. France was in decline.
5. The coalition partners adopted and followed a unified military strategy.

Napoleon was determined to fight on after the defeat in Russia and built up the remnant of his army to 400,000. By now the allies were aware of his tactics and in two heavily fought battles involving large numbers of men in eastern Germany in 1813, at Lutzen and Bautzen, he fought off his enemies but casualties were high on both sides. The scale of the war had escalated, with the allies (Russia, Prussia and Austria) fielding 800,000 men and France over 600,000. The Battle of Dresden was a French victory, but Napoleon found himself outnumbered at Leipzig in October 1813. Here, the so-called Battle of the Nations saw Napoleon wage an effective defensive battle, allowing him to withdraw into southern Germany where he defeated Bavaria and got back to France. Given the enormous difficulty and cost of finally defeating Napoleon, the allies offered peace proposals in November 1813. Austria and Prussia were anxious about Russian troops in Europe. France would have had to withdraw to her 'natural frontiers' but would still have kept Belgium, Savoy and the left bank of the Rhine.

Napoleon did not take up the offer and faced harsher terms in 1814, though these would still have left him in possession of France with the frontiers of 1791. He refused the 1814 terms too, which sealed his fate as he now faced an invasion of France. In the defensive campaigns of 1814 some of Napoleon's genius resurfaced but the problems of getting more troops were too much and internal divisions were now coming to the fore. There was no will among the Senate or the people for a long battle for the homeland.

The four major powers agreed the Treaty of Chaumont in March 1814. Its crucial outcome was the agreement not to make a separate peace but to continue fighting until Napoleon was defeated.

The collapse of the Empire

Back in France Napoleon struggled to gather and equip a new army. This was difficult as France was war-weary after twenty years of conscription. Finances were strained and people wanted peace. Napoleon resisted offers of negotiation and went on to win a number of small victories but was unable to stop the numerically superior advancing armies of the Sixth Coalition. As well as facing invasions by Austria, Prussia and Russia, France also faced invasion from the south by British forces from Spain under Wellington in 1814. Meanwhile he lost the political support of the Senate. By the end of March 1814 Paris had been occupied, Napoleon had abdicated and the Bourbon monarchy had been restored.

The Peace of Paris, 30 May 1814

By this treaty France was to lose all its territorial gains since 1792. Napoleon was exiled to the island of Elba with a pension. Meanwhile the four major powers, once united in war, began to fall out. Britain and Austria went so far as to make a secret alliance against Prussia and Russia.

Develop the detail

a

Below are a sample exam question and a paragraph written in answer to this question. The paragraph contains a limited amount of detail. Annotate the paragraph to add additional detail to the answer.

How important were the events of 1813–14 in the abdication of Napoleon?

Napoleon was still a significant force in Europe in 1813, but the events and decisions of 1813–14 were crucial in bringing about his abdication. Vital were key decisions he took not to accept peace terms. If he had accepted these, then he could still have been Emperor of France and he would have bought time to recover. Also important were the military events. Despite raising large forces, Napoleon could not win the decisive victories of his early campaigns against Austria and Prussia and he was driven back to France. Despite brilliant rearguard actions, it was clear that the French Senate and people no longer had the will for costly defences against foreign invasion.

Spectrum of importance

a

Below are a sample exam question and a list of general points which could be used to answer the question. Use your own knowledge and the information on the opposite page and page 72 to reach a judgement about the importance of these general points to the question posed. Write numbers on the spectrum below to indicate their relative importance. Having done this, write a brief justification of your placement, explaining why some of these factors are more important than others. The resulting diagram could form the basis of an essay plan.

Assess the reasons for the abdication of Napoleon in 1814.

1. The determination of the Sixth Coalition and the Treaty of Chaumont.
2. The Battle of Leipzig (the Battle of the Nations).
3. The invasion of France by its foreign enemies.
4. The refusal by Napoleon of peace terms.
5. The advances by Britain and Spanish forces in Spain and the invasion of southern France.
6. The heavy loss of life since 1812.

Least important reason ←——————————→ Most important reason

Napoleon's rule after 1807

REVISED

The Napoleonic Empire

By 1807 Napoleon was victorious, France dominated Europe, and the Empire was created. In the next four years smaller states were added until the Empire reached its greatest extent by 1811. It consisted of:

- France up to its 'natural frontiers' – the Alps, Pyrenees and River Rhine, including Belgium
- annexed territories – Piedmont (1802), Swiss Confederation (1803), Ligurian Republic (1805), Grand Duchy of Tuscany (1809)
- satellite states – kingdoms of Italy (1805), Naples (1806), Holland (1806), Westphalia (1807) and Spain (1808), the Confederation of the Rhine (1806) and the Grand Duchy of Warsaw (1807).

Thus 'France' had been considerably expanded.

The value and problems of the Napoleonic Empire

The annexed territories were treated as part of France with the same rights and obligations as any other region. Like them they provided tax income and soldiers.

The satellite states were treated differently. They were expected to pay tribute and to provide auxiliary soldiers for the Grande Armée. Members of Napoleon's family were placed on their thrones. This had the twin benefit of ensuring their loyalty and also rewarding his family. Finally, they were a useful source of lands and estates, taken from their original nobility or the Church, which Napoleon could give as rewards to his new nobility and to his leading marshals and generals.

The satellite states provided roughly half Napoleon's military expenditure in the decade 1804 to 1814, as well as financing the auxiliary troops that they had been forced to provide.

Problems

Conscription was hated and resisted. There was armed rebellion – in Naples, the Tyrol in Austria and Spain.

Such a large empire was difficult to control. Napoleon used members of his own family but there were only so many of them and not all were either competent or loyal. For example, Napoleon moved his brother Joseph from Naples to Spain and then replaced him with his brother-in-law, Marshall Murat. Murat later conspired against Napoleon. To the north Napoleon's brother Louis refused to implement the Continental System in Holland.

The control of the Empire: administration

The rulers of the satellite states were closely supervised by Napoleon and they were expected to rule in France's interests. Some changes were made to their administrative structures. They were divided into departments controlled by a prefect, just as in France.

Some of the smaller states in Germany and Italy were amalgamated or joined to bigger states. This has sometimes led to Napoleon being seen as a supporter of nationalism in countries other than France and as a contributor to the future growth of the states of Germany and Italy, but this was not his intention at the time.

The gendarmerie

One of Napoleon's key achievements was to impose law and order throughout France and gradually the Empire. Gendarmes, ex-soldiers, were stationed in units of six or seven men in small rural centres as well as in the towns. They were a visible presence of government and provided both protection and law and order.

Financial and economic policies

The reformed French taxation system served as a model throughout the Empire. Napoleon placed heavy financial demands on satellite states like Holland and Italy and, in order to meet these, they had to modernise their finances with more efficient tax collection and more careful state control.

However, considerable damage to local economies was caused by the burden of taxation, the economic destruction associated with warfare and French occupying troops. Moreover conscription removed manpower from agriculture and contributed to longer-term economic decline, as did the loss of men killed in Napoleon's battles.

Social policies

Napoleon did not abolish feudalism in all the territories he conquered. In some he adopted a practical approach of exercising his power through existing elites. Historians now agree that the groupings of nobles and bourgeoisie remained unchanged in much of Italy, Germany and Poland.

Support your judgement

Read the following sample exam question and two basic judgements. Support the judgement that you agree with most strongly by adding a reason and detail that justifies the judgement.
Tip: Whichever option you choose you will have to weigh up both sides of the argument. You could use words such as 'whereas' or 'although' in order to help the process of evaluation.

How much did Napoleon's rule of the Empire after 1807 benefit his subjects?

Napoleon gave his subjects stability and reform because ...

Napoleon merely exploited his imperial subjects because ...

Developing an argument

Below are a sample exam question, a list of key points to be made in the essay, and a paragraph from the essay. Read the question, the key points and the sample paragraph. Using the information from the opposite page and from page 68, rewrite the paragraph in order to develop an argument. Your paragraph should explain why the factor discussed in the paragraph is either the most significant factor or less significant than another factor.

'The interests of France dominated Napoleon's rule of his Empire.' Assess this view of Napoleon's imperial rule after 1807.

Key points:

- Heavy taxes.
- Conscription.
- Gendarmes were stationed to keep control.
- Annexed states had the same institutions and reforms as France.
- The rulers of annexed states were expected to rule in the interests of France.
- Napoleon gave important positions to his family members.
- French rule damaged local economies.
- The Empire enjoyed stability and administrative reforms.

Sample paragraph:

Napoleon's Empire had been achieved by conquest and depended on military power and an extensive police force. It was ruled in the interests of France, not the local people. Though the annexed lands were treated as part of France this meant that they had to meet the needs of Napoleon's rule. The satellite states were seen as sources of wealth and their resources were plundered. Napoleon's family members were imposed on them and it was made clear that they should rule in the interests of France. Administration was placed firmly under French control and not all the benefits of the French Revolution were passed on to the peoples of the Empire. Napoleon spoke of encouraging nationalism but, in the end, France came first.

The Hundred Days, 1815

REVISED

Napoleon's return

The Emperor had been exiled on the small island of Elba in 1814. When he saw that the allies were disagreeing about peace terms and also that the restored King **Louis XVIII** was becoming unpopular, he decided on a return. On 1 March 1815 he landed near Cannes with a thousand men and rapidly advanced north. He urged his old troops to rally to him and spoke about saving France from 'the priests and the nobles' by a second revolution. Troops sent under his old comrade Marshal Ney refused to arrest Napoleon and both they and Ney joined him. He progressed to Paris and Louis XVIII fled. By 20 March Napoleon was back in his old palace.

Napoleon expressed private doubts about a new constitution but held a mass rally to discuss reform. A new and more liberal constitution called the *Acte Additionnel* was proclaimed. It was known as 'le Benjamine' after its author, the writer and thinker Benjamin Constant. Napoleon claimed that he had always been a liberal, wanted more democracy and had worked for national freedom in Europe. He sent a message to the monarchs of Europe saying he wanted peace and accepting the Treaty of Paris.

Restarting the wars

The allies renewed their 1814 Treaty of Chaumont and tried to raise forces. Napoleon meanwhile recreated his army, calling on veterans. The allies had not expected such a rapid mobilisation and by 20 March he had 140,000 men with a 200,000 reserve. The main allied forces were in the Netherlands, with Wellington at Brussels and the Prussians under Blücher at Liège. Napoleon advanced against them, hoping to inflict defeats on them separately and discourage any further military action.

He had initial success against the Prussians. However, he failed to inflict a crushing defeat and detached part of his force under his subordinate, Grouchy, to pursue them and prevent any union with his next main enemy, the British. An initial encounter at Quatre Bras was indecisive and Wellington withdrew to Waterloo to defend Brussels. On 18 June the last great battle of the Napoleonic Wars took place. Despite all Napoleon's efforts on a rain-soaked battlefield he could not break Wellington's defences before the Prussians arrived. The British offered heroic resistance at the key points on the battlefield of Hougoumont and La Haye Sainte. Grouchy had failed to stop the Prussian forces joining the battle and Napoleon had failed in a series of unimaginative frontal assaults on Wellington's men.

Napoleon's abdication and second Treaty of Paris

While Napoleon wanted to continue the war, he lacked the political and popular support to do so. For a second time he had to abdicate on 22 June 1815 and this time the British took him into a more secure exile on the isolated island of St Helena. Meanwhile France lost more territory by the second Treaty of Paris, 20 November 1815.

The treatment of France by the Vienna settlement

In the final settlement negotiated at Vienna on 9 June 1815, the fate of the rest of Napoleon's Empire was decided. In some places the victors turned the clock back; in others they built upon the changes Napoleon had started. One key aim was to surround a weakened France with strong neighbours to prevent any future attempts at expansion.

Belgium was united with Holland to create a strong state to the north while in the south Spain was returned to its Bourbon rulers. Switzerland's independence was guaranteed. To the south-east a strengthened Kingdom of Sardinia–Piedmont was created and to the north-west the German Confederation was created.

Elsewhere Italian states were returned to Austrian influence or to their former rulers, such as the Pope in the Papal States and the Bourbons in Naples. Prussia gained control of a number of German states and Russia took most of Poland. The Empire was no more.

Simple essay style

Below is a sample exam question. Use your own knowledge, information on the opposite page and information from other sections of the book to produce a plan for this question. Choose four general points, and provide three pieces of specific information to support each general point. Once you have planned your essay, write the introduction and conclusion for the essay. The introduction should list the points to be discussed in the essay and outline the line of argument you intend to take. The conclusion should summarise the key points and justify which point was the most important.

Assess the reasons for the failure of the Hundred Days.

Eliminate irrelevance

a

Below are a sample exam question and a paragraph written in answer to this question. Read the paragraph and, using the information from the opposite page, identify parts of the paragraph that are not directly relevant to the question. Draw a line through the information that is irrelevant and justify your deletions in the margin.

Assess the view that the Hundred Days stood little chance of success.

Napoleon looked carefully at the divisions between the allies' powers at the Congress of Vienna and this encouraged him to risk another adventure. He arrived at the south of France and then moved northwards where he gained more and more support. A force sent against him did not follow orders to oppose him. He stepped forward and opened his coat, daring them to fire. The rapid flight of Louis XVIII and the limited resistance showed that the restored monarchy had a limited impact on the people. This was not the first daring adventure that Napoleon had undertaken in his career and he still believed that the same destiny that had seemed to guide him in Italy in 1796, in his bid to take power in 1799 or in the daring campaign of 1805 would lead to success. However, the new constitution was not much of an advance on the Charter given by Louis XVIII, and though Napoleon raised an army, too much was dependent on military success. Given the limited successes of his last campaigns, there was not much hope that he would remain in power simply by fighting some brilliant battles. Support drained away quickly and everything turned on the campaign in Belgium. But even if that had been successful, there was no certainty that the allies would have accepted Napoleon.

Napoleon's personal failings and reasons for his fall

REVISED

Napoleon's power depended on ongoing success. He was conscious that he had no real hereditary claim to the throne. There was little to hold a disparate empire together except his own power and prestige. From 1812, when failure became more common than success, Napoleon had no legitimacy to fall back on. There were several other factors.

War-weariness in France

By 1814 it was clear that the French people would not rally, as they had done during the Revolution, to defend the 'patrie', and also that there was a desire for peace and an end to the huge losses, both financial and human, that years of campaigning had brought about. The years of war had a devastating effect on French society. The death of over 900,000 young men in the armies was a great loss which also had a wider impact on society and future population growth. Economically, industries associated with the war effort, iron and textiles developed, as did trade with the rest of Europe. Inland areas on continental trading routes, such as Alsace on the River Rhine, prospered, while other areas, such as the maritime ports, suffered from the British blockade.

Military reasons

The enemies of Napoleon had reformed their tactics and organisation and increased the size of their armies. Napoleon's surprise tactics were no longer surprises. Also the nature of his armies changed after 1807. They were less composed of Frenchmen. Two-thirds comprised non-French conscripts or volunteers from the Empire. High casualties resulted in inferior troops having to be recruited and German, Dutch, Polish, Italian and Spanish soldiers did not make the army the cohesive force that it had been in the earlier period of Napoleon's victories. He had to rely less on skilful manoeuvre and more on forceful frontal attacks against troops which were not inferior, nor less inspired by loyalty or nationalism.

Changes among his enemies

By 1814 Napoleon's enemies were more united and determined. His failure to defeat Britain or overcome British sea supremacy meant that he had a determined and unconquerable enemy ready to finance coalitions against him. A strong sense of patriotism meant that Britain was prepared to support a long war, financially at least.

Nationalism

There was also the force of nationalism in Europe. Napoleon's invasions of Spain and Russia unleashed national feelings in those countries which made for heavy resistance. The 'Spanish ulcer' (see page 72) drained French resources and resulted in much costly guerrilla warfare. In Russia determined resistance led to scorched earth tactics which deprived Napoleon of supplies, and he met very costly resistance at the Battle of Borodino. Germany resented French rule and there was the development of a national opposition, though it was much less strong than in Spain.

Personal failings

Linked with all these factors are Napoleon's personal failings. The reverse of his determination and confidence was an obstinacy and failure to accept reality. He ignored warnings against invading Spain. He did not consider the problems of an invasion of Russia sufficiently and, perhaps most significant of all, he did not accept peace terms in 1813. Increasing lapses of judgement meant that he lost the confidence of some of his most able advisers like Fouché and **Talleyrand**, his foreign minister, who defected to his enemies. His devotion to his family also led to weaknesses at the heart of his Empire, as they were not always up to the huge responsibilities they faced. This was particularly true of his brother Joseph in Spain.

The bonds of affection with his armies had not been maintained and his troops often faced poor conditions and arrears of pay by the final campaigns.

Napoleon's health and physical condition also declined. This was particularly apparent in the Waterloo campaign – the crucial battle was conducted in an unimaginative and lacklustre way by a tired and overweight Napoleon. In the end everything was subordinated to the hopes of one outstanding military victory in 1815, which he failed to achieve.

Develop the detail

a

Below are a question and a paragraph written in answer to this question. The paragraph contains a limited amount of detail. Annotate the paragraph to add additional detail to the answer.

'The main reason for Napoleon's downfall was his personal failings.' How far do you agree?

> By 1812 the tide was turning against Napoleon. He had failed to defeat Britain or overcome its naval power. The huge losses of men and horses in Russia left his military power weakened and led to the powerful Sixth Coalition against him. However, it was essentially his egotism and lack of realism that led to his downfall. Rather than negotiate he went on to fight large-scale campaigns. He did not face the reality of his armies being weaker. He underestimated his enemies to the very end and he failed to maintain the loyalty of his most able supporters. He overestimated the willingness of France to support him.

Spectrum of importance

a

Below are a question and a list of general points which could be used to answer the question. Use your own knowledge and the information on pages 70, 72 and 74 to reach a judgement about the importance of these general points to the question posed. Write numbers on the spectrum below to indicate their relative importance. Having done this, write a brief justification of your placement, explaining why some of these factors are more important than others. The resulting diagram could form the basis of an essay plan.

Assess the reasons for the downfall of Napoleon.

1 British opposition
2 Development of greater unity among enemies
3 Bad decision-making regarding Spain and Russia
4 Failure to negotiate 1813
5 Changes in nature of French armies
6 War-weariness in France
7 Napoleon's personal exhaustion.

Least important reason ⟷ Most important reason

Exam focus

REVISED

Below are a exam-style question and a model answer. Read the question and then the answer and the comments around it.

'The strength of the Sixth Coalition was the decisive factor in the fall of Napoleon in 1814.' How far do you agree?

The agreement of Britain, Austria, Prussia and Russia to co-ordinate their military actions and stay together to defeat Napoleon was a major factor in Napoleon's defeat. To decide whether it was the decisive factor needs to be considered in the light of other factors. These were: the lessons members of the Sixth Coalition had learned from their earlier failures, the crucial mistakes that Napoleon made in invading Spain in 1808 and Russia in 1812 and the weaknesses in his position in France and in his Empire and his own overwhelming confidence in his abilities to defeat his enemies. Though the unity of his enemies was a major factor it was his own inability to realise his own limitations and the changes in warfare since 1807 that were more important.

> There is a clear introduction which appears balanced with recognition there were a series of factors.

> The opening paragraph offers a clear view of the line of argument that the candidate will take.

The Sixth Coalition against Napoleon consisted of Britain, Austria, Prussia and Russia and it had a number of key advantages over earlier coalitions which gave it its strength. First its members had a common aim, to free Germany from French control. Second all four major powers were a part of it. Third they agreed to follow a unified military strategy. Fourth all had improved their armies with better artillery, more flexible troop formations and new generals and tactics. They had more effectively mobilised for war. Crucially in March 1814 they agreed the Treaty of Chaumont. By its terms they agreed not to make a separate peace with Napoleon but to stay at war until he had been defeated. Despite enduring some heavy losses in 1813 and 1814, the coalition held together more than the Third and Fourth Coalitions had. In the previous wars against Napoleon the coalitions had tended to fail to act together.

> Importantly, the key element in the question is addressed and reasons why the coalition could be decisive are given.

> The explanation is developed.

Previous coalitions had been weak and Napoleon had been able to exploit this. However, by 1813 the European powers had learnt from their mistakes. The lack of co-ordination between Austria and Russia which had been so disastrous in 1805 was not repeated. Countries did not make separate treaties with Napoleon as Austria did after Austerlitz. The Prussian military reforms had adopted some of the key ideas of Napoleon and the French armies. Napoleon's tactics were well known, and at Leipzig, for instance, he was not able to produce any surprising, decisive military tactics against a weak enemy that had been such a feature of his successes before 1807.

> Comparisons with earlier coalitions are made and the argument is well developed.

However, to see the strengths of the coalition in isolation would be to overestimate them. The army they faced was not the strong and largely French force of the earlier wars. The heavy losses in Russia of men, equipment and especially horses had weakened the Emperor. Also the long years of warfare in Spain had drained his resources. He himself saw the Peninsular War as the 'Spanish ulcer'. The defeats there and the long and costly retreat from Russia had ended a powerful element in Napoleon's military success, the belief in his invincibility and destiny. In addition, his failure to defeat Britain by the Continental System and the weak naval strategy had left Britain free to continue to unify Europe against him and to supply the coalition with large subsidies.

> The opening sentence of this paragraph introduces a counter-argument.

> The counter-argument is developed.

Resources had swung in favour of his enemies since 1812 when Napoleon was able to take 600,000 men into Russia. This was important because war had changed. Increasingly, it became a matter not of master strokes but of pitched battles such as Borodino where numbers were important and in the end that, rather than the strength of a coalition, would count against Napoleon. However, it was not necessarily the strength of his enemies' resources, their unity, the British subsidies or their determination which ensured Napoleon's downfall. After Russia he was still a formidable force, able to gather large armies and inflict heavy casualties on his opponents. Neither Spain nor Russia had brought him to his knees. Also the European powers were not entirely united. Austria and Prussia did not see the prospect of growing Russian power without some concern. Though they were not prepared to accept the great Empire that Napoleon had created they were prepared to accept peace terms which would allow France to keep some of its post-1792 gains. The ongoing costs of war were considerable and Napoleon was still a dangerous opponent. However, Napoleon's whole career was based on self-confidence and a belief in destiny and it was this that let him down. He had not created loyalty or unity in his Empire and in France itself his frequent absences, the heavy costs of his campaigns and the lack of successes since 1809 had lost him vital support. His failure to realise that by 1814 the nation would not rally to the 'fatherland in danger' as it had in 1792–93 led him into fatal miscalculation. It was not so much the strength of the coalition as his personal failings and arrogance that led to his downfall.

A key point in the introduction is developed and a judgement made.

The judgement is now developed further and the view in the introduction is explained.

A challenge is made to the idea of allied unity.

A very clear judgement is made which links to the view in the introduction. The answer has taken the reader through the case for the coalition and then argued against it.

The answer is well focused and wide-ranging. The level of supporting knowledge is good and it is used to take the argument forward, rather than simply imparting it. There are judgements about the issues discussed and an overall judgement, which follows from the argument in the main body of the essay, is reached. As a result the answer would reach the higher levels of the mark bands.

Characteristics of a strong period study essay

You have now considered four sample high-level essays. Use these essays to make a bullet-pointed list of the characteristics of a strong period study essay. Use this list when planning and writing your own practice exam essays.

Exam focus

REVISED

Below are an exam-style question and sample short answer. Read the question and then the answer and the comments around it.

Which was more important in the failure of Napoleon's war against Britain?

i The Peninsular War

ii The Battle of Waterloo

The Peninsular War was the most drawn-out of Napoleon's campaigns and contributed a great deal to his eventual failure. When he left Spain his armies had only limited success without his leadership. Wellington could not be dislodged from his defences near Lisbon. The force of nationalism in Spain was strong and there were heavy casualties from guerrilla warfare. The war was the first major indication that France could be beaten; large number of troops were held down in the war and were not available for other campaigns. The war showed Napoleon's weakness in sea power as Wellington could be supplied by sea. It took resources and reduced French prestige. It also encouraged ongoing attempts to defeat Britain by economic warfare, which had bad effects on Europe. Napoleon's family lost prestige as Joseph struggled to deal with a people he could not control. All this gave Britain encouragement to maintain opposition against him. It also gave Britain a battleground where its armies could engage with those of France with increasing success, culminating in the invasion of southern France in 1814, increasing Britain's prestige in Europe and providing Wellington with the experience that he would use in Napoleon's final defeat in 1815.

The significance of the war is stated.

Reasons for its importance are stated and fully explained.

A further reason for its importance is explained and a useful link with Waterloo is made.

The Battle of Waterloo was of huge importance in the final defeat of Napoleon in 1815 during the Hundred Days. After taking control of the state it was important for Napoleon to persuade the other European powers to accept his return. To do this he decided to attack his main enemies before they could unite and his initial success in defeating Prussian forces allowed him to concentrate on Wellington's army. Wellington was forced into a drawn-out and costly defensive battle. Without the British forces' defence of the chateau at Hougoumont and the farm of La Haye Sainte then Napoleon would have achieved the decisive victory which might have swung the diplomatic balance and persuaded the French people that the Hundred Days was more than a temporary and dangerous episode. Alongside French errors in not following up the victory against Blücher and the ability of the Prussian leader to arrive at the battlefield in time to drive off Napoleon's forces, British troops played a key role in the defeat of Napoleon.

The significance of Waterloo is explained.

There is a touch of balance.

The Peninsular War was fought at a time when Napoleon had enormous authority throughout Europe but Waterloo was fought at a time when that authority had been lost and it was doubtful whether Napoleon had enough support in France or any real chance of persuading the allies to accept his return. Thus the significance of the Peninsular War was greater. By questioning French military power and by unleashing forces of nationalism against Napoleon, the war began the whole collapse of the Napoleonic Empire. When Napoleon was in exile, he himself saw this and not Waterloo as the key element in his failure. The existence of the ongoing struggle in Spain encouraged British-subsidised resistance by Austria in 1809 and also encouraged the key Sixth Coalition against Napoleon. Without this, then Napoleon would not have needed to return in 1815 and might have maintained his power. Napoleon was a much more formidable opponent in 1808–14 than in 1815, and as the British in Spain were

There is a clear view of relative significance.

Comparison is sustained.

so important in undermining his position, then it is the Peninsular War that is more important. Waterloo was very significant but it defeated an already weak Emperor and even if Wellington had been defeated there was no certainty that Napoleon would have remained in power; thus the Peninsular War is of greater significance.

The judgement is confirmed.

The comparison in the final paragraph leads to an overall conclusion being reached.

The significance of the two issues is thoroughly analysed and explained using detailed own knowledge. The final paragraph compares their importance in a balanced fashion before reaching an overall judgement. Although there is more that could be said, the answer, in the time allowed, reaches a convincing judgement and would reach the top level.

Using other knowledge

In these short-answer essays there is a great deal of information that could be used, but does not appear in the response because of the constraints of time. Write your own response to this question, trying to use other knowledge of events.

Glossary

Absenteeism Higher clergy like bishops not living in their dioceses as they were pursuing a political career at court.

Absolute monarch An absolute monarch is one who has no legal limits to their power over their subjects.

American colonies British colonies in North America declared independence from Britain in 1776 and, in the resulting war between them and the British government, France fought on the side of the colonists.

Anglo-American War of 1812 A war between Britain and the USA that lasted until 1815. It was prompted by British trade restrictions as part of the naval blockade of France, the seizure of hundreds of US sailors for the Royal Navy and tensions in North America.

Assignats Bonds backed up by the sale of Church land that circulated as a form of paper money.

Battle of Trafalgar Key British naval victory in which Admiral Nelson destroyed the combined French and Spanish fleets, thus securing control of the seas.

Billeted When soldiers are lodged in people's houses, which was greatly resented in France.

Bourgeoisie Originally meaning 'the citizens of a town', by 1789 the term described the middle classes. These included merchants, industrialists, business people, financiers, landowners, doctors, lawyers and civil servants.

Black market Illegal internal trade to avoid duties or a ban on certain goods.

Brigands Gangs of robbers operating in areas where the forces of law and order were weak.

Cahiers de doléances The lists of grievances and suggestions for reform drawn up by the three orders for the meeting of the Estates General.

Catechism A summary of Christian teaching in the form of questions and answers.

Chouans Royalist rebels in western France who were usually peasants.

Commissions Military or naval officer posts had to be bought. Therefore all officers were nobles.

Committee of General Security (CGS) A committee of National Convention deputies that kept a watch on state security and foreign agents.

Committee of Public Safety (CPS) A committee of National Convention deputies that came to be a war cabinet.

Commune Municipal government of Paris.

Conscription The compulsory enrolment of men into the armed forces.

Constitutional monarchy Political system where the powers of the monarch are limited by a constitution.

Court factions Groupings of nobles at court, including the Queen and the King's brothers, who pursued policies that benefited them or that they approved of.

Citizens' militia A defence force composed of bourgeois Parisians set up to protect property. It later became the National Guard.

Civisme Good citizenship; being a good citizen.

Curé The parish priest, who in the countryside was often the only educated person in the village and was highly influential among the peasants.

Dauphin The heir to the French throne.

Dechristianisation The movement to destroy the French Catholic Church and the practice of religion.

Deflation A general reduction in prices in an economy.

Departments The divisions of France for elections and local government introduced in 1790.

Despot A monarch or ruler who exercises absolute power, especially in a cruel or oppressive way.

Dry guillotine The term used to describe the punishment of exile to the French colony of Guiana as so many exiles died of tropical diseases.

Émigrés These were nobles who had emigrated from France since the Revolution began, including Louis' brothers. Their activities, such as calling on foreign rulers for military help, increased fears of counter-revolution.

Enragés Insulting term, 'the angry ones', used to describe militants.

Estates General A body containing representatives of all three estates of France – Church, nobility and Third Estate – called in times of national emergency. It last met in 1614.

Farmers-General The syndicate of men who every six years contracted with the crown to collect certain taxes such as the *taille*. With a staff of roughly 30,000 they were the largest employer in France after the King's army and navy.

Fédérés Provincial National Guards.

Feudalism/Feudal rights System by which peasants held land in return for some of their labour and their produce. Landowners had control of manorial courts, exclusive rights to hunting and fishing, and the right to have a dovecote and the monopoly of operating mills, ovens and wine presses.

Garde Francaise These were units of the French army stationed in Paris to maintain order. Harsh discipline and contacts with the people of Paris brought discontent and some of the Garde joined the attack on the Bastille.

Généralités Thirty-six administrative regions into which Ancien Régime France was divided.

Girondins A small group of deputies from the Gironde area and their associates; most notable was Brissot.

Grapeshot Ammunition consisting of a number of small iron balls fired together from a cannon.

Guerrilla warfare Irregular warfare carried out by the people of an area against larger regular armies.

Indulgents The faction led by Danton who campaigned for an end to the Terror in early 1794.

Intendant Ancien Régime royal official in charge of a *généralité*.

Jacobins The name given to Dominican monks in Paris. When the Breton deputies began to hold their meetings in the Jacobins' former convent they were mockingly called Jacobins by their opponents in the National Assembly, suggesting they were like monks.

Journée A day of popular action and disturbance linked to great political change, such as the storming of the Bastille.

Justice of the Peace A new official based on the English model. JPs were elected by active citizens, one per canton, to serve for two years making judgements on cases up to the value of 50 livres.

Laissez faire A policy of non-interference by governments in the workings of the economy.

Lit de justice A formal session of a parlement during which the monarch could forcibly register an edict overriding the parlement's objections.

Livres The livre was the basic currency of France until 7 April 1795; 1 louis = 24 livres, 1 livre = 20 sous, 1 sou = 12 deniers.

Masonic Lodges These were local secret societies which were set up to fund charities but more importantly were places where men could debate the new ideas about society and government. Between 1773 and 1779 over 20,000 men joined.

Montagnards Those National Convention deputies who sat on the high benches to the left of the chair, the 'Mountain'.

Neo-Jacobins New Jacobins, the left-wing group who emerged after Thermidor.

Parlement High courts of appeal that combined legal and administrative functions. All edicts from the crown had to be ratified by the parlements before they could be enforced. There were thirteen in 1789 of which the parlement of Paris was most important.

Partage A system of inheritance in which an estate was divided equally among all the male heirs.

Physiocrats Economists who believed that the wealth of the nation came solely from agriculture and that all state regulations, tolls and price controls should be ended.

Plebiscite A popular vote on a single issue; it was a feature of Napoleon's France that allowed him to appeal over the heads of the political classes directly to the people. Today we might use the term referendum.

Pluralism Some higher clergy held more than one diocese and rarely visited them.

Poor relief Payments of food given to the poor by the Catholic Church.

Prefects Officials placed in charge of a department in Napoleonic France.

Princes of the Blood The King's seven closest male relatives, including his brothers, the Comte de Provence and the Comte d'Artois, and cousin Louis, Duc D'Orléans.

Ratified Formally approved before becoming officially valid.

Red Cap of Liberty This pointed red cap was a popular form of headwear in the Revolution. It was based on the hat worn by the ancient Phrygians and seen as a symbol of liberty.

Refractory clergy Those clergy who refused to swear an oath of loyalty to the constitution.

Representatives on mission National Convention deputies sent to the provinces, two to each, and to the armies to make sure government policy was followed. They had wide-reaching powers.

Royal patronage The King's power to grant lands, give offices and give money as a reward to courtiers.

Salon An event hosted in her home by an aristocratic woman to which she would invite a range of guests, nobles and bourgeoisie, to discuss art, literature and politics.

Sans-culottes The name coined in 1791 for the small property owners, shop-keepers and workers, both masters and their employees, who came out in support of the Revolution. They were not the poor. Nor were they a rabble, as portrayed and demonised by their opponents. Sans-culottes translates as 'without breeches', the label suggesting they were trouser-wearing workers rather than bourgeois or nobles in silk stockings and breeches. After the Revolution they disappeared as a group from French history.

Scorched earth A military strategy of destroying everything in an area that might be useful to an enemy.

Séance royale A Royal Session of the Estates General attended by all three estates.

Seigneur The lord of a manor who held seigneurial or feudal rights over the peasants.

Seigneurial courts These were law courts run by seigneurs who had legal jurisdiction over peasants.

Seven Years' War (1756–63) France, in alliance with Austria, was defeated by Britain and Prussia. One reason for France intervening in the American War of Independence was the chance for revenge on Britain.

Stipends A regular fixed sum paid as a salary to a churchman.

Subsistence farming Growing enough food to feed yourself and your family with nothing left over for sale.

Tax farming Employing private individuals or companies to collect state taxes in return for a share of the income.

Terrorists The name given to Robespierre and his associates after Thermidor, putting the blame for the Terror on them.

Tithe A tax paid to the Church of one-tenth of annual produce.

Universal suffrage Voting by all adults.

Venal office An official job or post that could be bought, which gave its holder noble status.

Veto A constitutional right to reject a proposal by a law-making body.

Key figures

Louis XVI (1754–93, King of France 1774–92) Inherited the throne from his grandfather Louis XV. While he was successful in the American War of Independence he never resolved the financial problems of the crown. He failed to follow a consistent course in the early stages of the Revolution and the flight to Varennes lost him much popularity. Following the failure of constitutional monarchy, for which he was in part responsible, he was overthrown, imprisoned, tried and executed for treason.

Marie Antoinette (1755–93, Queen of France 1774–92) Austrian-born Queen of France. She damaged the prestige of the monarchy with her alleged extravagance and involvement in scandals. She opposed compromise with the revolutionaries and pursued the full restoration of Louis XVI's powers. She was viewed as head of the shadowy Austrian Committee and did pass military information to the Austrians in 1792.

Louis XVIII (1755–1824) Louis, Count of Provence, was the brother of Louis XVI. He went into exile in 1791 and after the death of Louis XVI's son was heir; he was restored by the allies as King Louis XVIII in 1814. Though he accepted that he was constitutional monarch, he was driven out by Napoleon during the Hundred Days and restored a second time. He ruled with varying degrees of success until 1824.

Napoleon Bonaparte (1769–1821, Emperor of France 1804–14 and 1814–15) Son of a Corsican lawyer who trained for the army in France and rose to high command during the Revolution. Under the Directory his brilliant victories in Italy gave him the popularity to be able to seize power in the Coup of Brumaire. Thereafter he ruled France as Consul and then Emperor until his forced abdication in 1815.

Jacques Pierre Brissot (1754–93) A journalist and pamphleteer who spoke regularly at the Jacobin Club. He was a member of the Legislative Assembly and associated with the Girondins. He was influential in the decision for war in 1792. A member of the Convention, he opposed the execution of the King. He was arrested, tried and guillotined in 1793 by his Jacobin opponents.

Georges-Jacques Danton (1759–94) Lawyer who emerged as an early leader of the Cordeliers. He was involved in the overthrow of Louis XVI. Appointed Minister of Justice of the Provisional Executive Committee, he failed to prevent the September massacres but did rally the capital for the war effort. He was an early member of the CPS before retiring in ill health. Returned to politics to campaign for an end to the Terror to which he fell victim.

Camille Desmoulins (1760-1794) Trained as a lawyer but was influenced by the events of 1789 to become a radical journalist and politician. His impromptu oratory stirred up crowds in July 1789. He supported the ideas of Danton and Robespierre but fell foul of faction struggles. He and his wife were executed in April 1794 after a break with Robespierre.

Joseph Fouché, Duke of Otranto (1759–1820) National Convention deputy sent as a representative on mission to Lyons where he organised the *mitraillades* (severe repression and mass shootings). Threatened by Robespierre, he helped plot Thermidor before dropping out of politics until he became Minister of Police in 1799, a role he continued in under Napoleon.

Jacques-René Hébert (1757–94) Began publishing the radical journal, *Le Père Duchesne*, in September 1790. He was active in the Cordeliers Club and in the Paris Commune and the overthrow of Louis XVI. A radical thinker, he continually argued for more Terror as well as being part of the dechristianisation movement. Following his attacks on the Indulgents he was arrested and convicted on trumped-up charges.

Jean-Paul Marat (1744–93) Radical revolutionary journalist implicated in the September massacres. His impeachment was a key factor in the fall of the Girondins. His assassination by Charlotte Corday in part triggered the Terror.

Jacques Necker (1732–1804) Genevan banker who served as finance minister, 1777–81. His second spell in government (1788–89) was unsuccessful. He mishandled the Estates General and was in Switzerland when the fall of the Bastille forced Louis to recall him. He was marginalised by the workings of the Constituent Assembly and emigrated in 1790.

Marquis de Lafayette (1757–1834) Liberal noble who fought in the American War of Independence. Appointed commander of the new Parisian National Guard but lost popularity for his support of constitutional monarchy and his part in the Champs de Mars massacre. As a revolutionary general he tried to turn his army on Paris and when that failed defected to the enemy. Returned to live in France under Napoleon.

Maximilien Robespierre (1758–94) Son of a lawyer who came to national prominence having been elected to the Estates General in 1789. He was very influential in the Jacobin Club and instrumental in the overthrow and execution of the King, and acted as spokesman for the Committee of Public Safety on which he served 1793 to 1794 when he was guillotined.

Jean-Jacques Rousseau (1712–78) One of the leading *philosophes*, who wrote among other works *The Social Contract*. He argued that a despotic monarch could be overthrown by their subjects and that sovereignty resided in the people rather than in the person of the King. His ideas were very influential among many revolutionaries including Robespierre and Madame Roland.

Abbé Sieyès (1748–1836) Emmanuel-Joseph Sieyès was born into a bourgeois family, trained for the Church and was ordained in 1773. Influenced by Rousseau he supported reform. He wrote the pamphlet *What is the Third Estate?*, served as a deputy to the Estates General, and helped draw up the Tennis Court Oath and the Rights of Man. Thereafter his influence waned. A supporter of constitutional monarchy he voted for the death of the King but kept a low profile during the Terror. After Robespierre's fall he regained influence and plotted the Coup of Brumaire. Outmanoeuvred by Napoleon, he retired from public life.

Charles Talleyrand (1754–1838) Talleyrand was a bishop in 1789 when he entered the Estates General as a deputy but renounced it after the Civil Constitution of the Clergy. He was exiled after the overthrow of the monarchy but returned to serve as foreign minister under the Directory, then Napoleon and then the restored Bourbons.

Timeline

1774 Accession of Louis XVI

1776 Turgot appointed finance minister

1777 Necker appointed finance minister

1778 France entered the American War of Independence against Britain

1781 Necker resigned

1783 Peace of Paris ended American War of Independence

Calonne appointed finance minister

1787 Meeting of the Assembly of Notables

1788 Estates General called for 1789

Payments from the Treasury suspended

Second Assembly of Notables

Royal decree to double the number of Third Estate deputies

1789 Opening of the Estates General at Versailles

National Assembly claimed national sovereignty

Tennis Court Oath

Fall of the Bastille

The Great Fear in the countryside

Declaration of the Rights of Man

October Days, royal family brought back to Paris

1790 Feudalism abolished

Civil Constitution of the Clergy

1791 Flight to Varennes

Champs de Mars massacre

Pillnitz Declaration by Austrian and Prussian monarchs

1792 War declared on Austria

Publication of the Brunswick Manifesto

Overthrow of the monarchy

1793 Trial and execution of Louis XVI

Revolutionary Tribunal created

Revolt in the Vendée began

Committee of Public Safety created

Federalist revolts – Bordeaux, Caen and Lyons

Levée en masse decree issued

Girondins executed

1794 Hébertists executed

Dantonists executed

The Law of Prairial

Thermidor; fall of Robespierre

End of the Terror

1795 White Terror in southern France

Vendémiaire uprising in Paris – Whiff of Grapeshot

Directory inaugurated

1796 Napoleon appointed commander of Italian campaign

1797 Napoleon agreed Treaty of Campo Formio with Austria

1798 Napoleon's Egyptian campaign

1799 War of the Second Coalition

Coup of Brumaire – Bonaparte took power

Bonaparte First Consul

1800 Bank of France founded

Napoleon won Battle of Marengo

Failed assassination attempt on Napoleon

1801 Concordat with the Pope

1802 Peace of Amiens, end of Revolutionary Wars

Tribunate purged for opposing the Civil Code

Plebiscite confirmed Napoleon as First Consul for Life

1803 Britain declared war on France, start of Napoleonic Wars, War of the Third Coalition

1804 Execution of the Duc d'Enghien

Civil Code promulgated

Napoleon crowned Emperor

1805 Napoleon crowned King of Italy in Milan

Third Coalition formed

Naval defeat at Trafalgar ended any hope of invading Britain

Napoleon won the Battle of Austerlitz against Austrians and Russians

1806 Creation of the Confederation of the Rhine

War of the Fourth Coalition

Napoleon defeated Prussians at Battle of Jena

1807 Napoleon defeated the Russians at the Battles of Eylau and Friedland

Treaty of Tilsit

Creation of the Kingdom of Westphalia and the Duchy of Poland

Napoleonic Code – Civil Code – was introduced to other areas of Europe

1808 Peninsular War began

Legislature abolished

1809 War of the Fifth Coalition

1810 Napoleon divorced Joséphine and married Marie-Louise of Austria

1812 Britain and the USA were at war

Napoleon invaded Russia

Retreat from Moscow

1813 Sixth Coalition formed

Napoleon defeated at Battle of Leipzig (Battle of the Nations) by an army of Austrians, Prussians and Russians

1814 Treaty of Chaumont, formal alliance of the great powers – Austria, Britain, Prussia and Russia

Paris surrendered, Talleyrand head of provisional government

First Bourbon Restoration

First Treaty of Paris

Napoleon exiled to Elba

Congress of Vienna opened

1815 The 'Hundred Days'

Battle of Waterloo

Napoleon's abdication

Second Bourbon Restoration

Napoleon landed in St Helena

1821 Napoleon died in exile

Answers

Page 9

Turning assertion into argument

The first two estates had too much privilege because … the clergy held 10 per cent of the land but comprised only 0.5 per cent of the population and the nobles, though only 1 per cent of the population, owned a third to a quarter of the land and dominated office holding. They also enjoyed tax exemption.

The peasantry was particularly harmed because … of the burdens of feudal dues and labour services.

Middle-class grievances were important because … the middle classes were growing in numbers and wealth but lacked the privileges of the first two estates.

Page 11

Delete as applicable

It can be seen as both fair and unfair (unfair in the sense that he inherited problems and was not uncaring/fair in the sense that he lacked decisiveness and dynamism) to argue that Louis was in himself an inadequate king. The limits on his power in practice were considerable. The system of government he inherited was not very efficient and weak. France itself was divided and under central control. However, the royal intendants faced opposition. Louis' popularity was hindered by his marriage to Marie Antoinette. The King himself took an interest in affairs of state. An important part of his view of kingship was his belief in traditional privileges.

Page 13

Introducing an argument

The introduction does not assess the importance of the problems but just describes them.

The conclusion needs to say why finance was the most pressing problem and offer a view about the relative importance of the other factors.

Develop the detail

Possible additions: examples of royal ministers; examples of reforms; examples of opposition to reform; names of special assemblies.

Page 15

Challenge the historian

1 Ford is arguing that there was no specific Enlightenment programme and that its importance was that it led to a critical attitude.

2 Anti-religious views of Voltaire questioned Church authority. Montesquieu questioned institutions of government.

3 Some ideas went beyond simply questioning institutions, e.g. Rousseau's ideas of popular sovereignty.

Page 17

Support your judgement

Economic hardship could be seen as the most fundamental because it affected the peasantry, who were the bulk of the population, and the rise in food prices caused discontent in important urban centres like Paris.

It could be argued that social factors were the most important because social discontent was long term while economic conditions might improve with better harvests. The resentments of the middle classes and long-term dislike of feudal burdens were likely to get worse.

Page 19

Develop the detail

There could be an explanation of the social grievances, the resentments in society could be exemplified and the political factors should be explained.

Page 23

Develop the detail

Answer could explain briefly why the storming of the Bastille was the greatest revolutionary act and what consequences it had, and why the Declaration of the Rights of Man was so important, but the biggest need is to link changes to the popular unrest more.

Challenge the historian

1 The interpretation suggests that the key turning point was 4 August because it had a decisive impact on the ancient regime and led to other changes.

2 Could mention the end of feudalism and class barriers.

3 Might suggest that the forming of a National Assembly was more significant or that, though these were social changes, other political changes were less drastic.

Page 25

Introducing an argument

There could be a more decisive judgement here and the events could be linked more to the argument that the King could not survive.

The conclusion needs to explain why, despite all the developments, the King was not doomed by October 1789 and why the constitutional monarchy might have worked.

RAG – Rate the timeline

February 1787	The Assembly of Notables met
August 1788	Brienne agreed that the Estates General should meet
April 1789	The Réveillon riots
May 1789	The Estates General met
17 June 1789	The National Assembly formed
20 June 1789	The Tennis Court Oath
11 July 1789	The National Assembly became the National Constituent Assembly
14 July 1789	The storming of the Bastille
20 July 1789	Start of the Great Fear
4 August 1789	Assembly voted to end feudalism
26 August 1789	The Declaration of the Rights of Man
5 October 1789	Paris crowds marched on Versailles
6 October 1789	The royal family brought to Paris

Page 31

Delete as applicable

The reforms of 1789–91 made big changes to many aspects of French life. Local government was changed radically. Changes to the Church were highly significant. This led to considerable opposition. The new state had some democratic elements because of the distinction between active and passive citizens. The new justice system was important in ending the power of the nobles.

Identify an argument

Sample 2 has more judgements and supported argument.

Page 33

Turning assertion into argument

The King's flight to Varennes made it impossible for any future constitutional monarchy to work because … the King was seen to oppose the new regime and to seek to join its enemies.

Though important, the flight to Varennes did not necessarily mean that the constitution of 1791 would fail because … when he returned he was not imprisoned but continued to rule as constitutional monarch.

Page 35

Developing an argument

This answer deals with the importance of popular action but not its importance relative to other factors. More judgement is needed.

Page 37

Develop the detail

It is not clear what the long- and short-term factors were so the King's failure to either accept or suppress the Revolution needs explaining, Also why the war was so important needs expansion.

Page 39

Spectrum of importance

Many will think that the war is connected to many of the other factors, so that 5 might be most important, and 7 is more a trigger than a fundamental cause but there is no correct answer.

Turning Assertion into Argument

The war was the key factor in bringing about the Terror because … in 1793 France was fighting much of Europe and the Revolution had to be defended. The Committee of Public Safety had been formed to coordinate the war effort and executed 84 generals such was the importance of winning the war.

Counter Revolution was more important than war in bringing about the Terror … because more people were executed in the provinces as a result of revolts than in Paris. In Vendée 8,700 were killed as opposed to 2,639 in Paris showing how important it was to crush counter revolution.

Page 41

Spot the mistake

This gives a view of Robespierre but does not engage with the key idea of 'dictatorial'.

Page 43

Complete the paragraph

The Thermidorian regime was established as a result of a violent coup against extremists. Though it was a relief to many in the Convention, as well as in the country as a whole, that the power of Robespierre and the Terrorists had been broken, France still faced many problems. Though no longer as dangerous as at the height of the Terror, France still faced foreign opposition and internal rebellion. There were ongoing financial problems and there were risings not only in the provinces but also in Paris itself. The Thermidorian regime was therefore highly unstable and as time went on it became more and more dependent on military power to keep control.

Develop the detail

The paragraph could explain the 'emergency conditions', i.e. the defeats in war; the reason for the contempt for the religious policies, i.e. the Cult of the Supreme Being could be explained; the reference to deaths could be expanded with the danger that Robespierre wanted to turn on his critics in the Committee and Convention.

Page 45

Introducing an argument

The introduction needs a clearer judgement on how serious the problems were – the inflation, for example, had been controlled and the insurrections in Paris suppressed.

The conclusion needs a judgement – despite solving some problems, was there an underlying instability and over-dependence on military force?

Page 51

Support your judgement

Ruthlessness and overwhelming ambition characterised the rise of Napoleon … as in the suppression of the insurrection in Paris and his obvious ambitions to gain glory in Italy and Egypt.

Ruthlessness and ambition alone could not have led to the rise to prominence of Napoleon: … he depended on the opportunities opened up by the Revolution and the patronage, support and military ideas of others.

Page 53

Turning assertion into argument

Napoleon's own military abilities were the key reason for his early success as a general because … he showed decisive leadership in Italy and was prepared to move rapidly, live off the land and win the support of his troops.

However, in many instances, he faced weak enemies, as in Italy where … his enemies were not prepared for rapid movement.

Also, in Egypt, Napoleon did not face modern forces because … they lacked modern artillery.

Page 55

Use own knowledge to support or contradict

Summary: Barnett stresses the favourable circumstances with rebellion, bankruptcy and the desire for a strong man to save the Republic. The crisis rather than Napoleon's own abilities seems to be the key.

This could be supported by knowledge of royalist revolts and also the danger from the neo-Jacobins.

It could be contradicted by stressing the leadership abilities that Bonaparte had shown in Italy and the way that he had become thought of as the man to save the Republic.

Page 57

Support or challenge?

	Support	Challenge
He set up prefects in the 83 departments.	X	
In 1802 Napoleon became Consul for Life.	X	
Napoleon held plebiscites on major issues.		X
There was a new legal code for the whole of France.		X
The abolition of feudalism was confirmed.		X
The authority of fathers and husbands over women was strengthened.	X	
The Tribunate could discuss laws but not vote and the Senate could vote but not discuss laws.	X	
The male population could vote.		X
The male population voted for a list of electors who in turn voted for another list of electors for the Tribunate.	X	

Delete as applicable

The codification of all laws into a single code was a very important development. It established that all citizens should have civil rights and equal justice so this showed that the work of the Revolution was being continued. The Code was popular for property owners. The Code was partly liberal. The Code was unfavourable for the position of women. Divorce law made men and women unequal. The Code reflected Napoleon's own ideas on authority and discipline to a large extent.

Page 59

Developing an argument

The paragraph needs an overall judgement rather than just saying there were some benefits. Napoleon was also concerned with his own power.

Page 61

Use own knowledge to support or contradict

Summary: The interpretation places emphasis on Napoleon's own abilities as a military genius – his skills of rapid movement, his understanding of topography and how to use artillery, and his leadership qualities.

Agree: This can be seen in his rapid movement in 1805 to outmanoeuvre the Austrians at Ulm and his tactics at Austerlitz.

Contradict: His genius was not always apparent, as at Marengo in 1800, and depended a lot on the errors of others, for example Mack at Ulm and Alexander I at Austerlitz.

Page 69

Develop the detail

'Economic warfare' could be explained – i.e. cutting off British exports. The aims and nature of the Continental System could be explained. The consequences for other countries, especially in the restriction of British colonial products and raw materials, could be developed.

Page 71

Eliminate irrelevance

The explanations of Napoleon's 1805 land campaign and the war in Spain are not necessary.

Page 73

Turning assertion into argument

The defeat in Russia meant that Napoleon was put on the road to eventual ruin because … of the loss of prestige and the heavy losses of men and horse. The war led to a renewed coalition against him.

However, the war in Spain was seen by Napoleon himself as more important because … it was so drawn out and was a constant drain on resources.

Yet it was not as important because … even after the defeat Napoleon could have made peace and Russian victory worried Austria.

Page 75

Develop the detail

The events of 1813–14 could be developed. The nature of the peace terms could be explained, showing that they were quite reasonable given the losses Napoleon had incurred. The military events could be specified, e.g. the Battle of the Nations.

Spectrum of importance

Many might think that 1 is the most significant as Napoleon had previously been able to weaken coalitions against him. There is no set answer.

Page 77

Support your judgement

Napoleon gave his subjects stability and reform because … in France he ended the revolutionary upheavals and gave his European subjects the benefits of codified law and better government.

Napoleon merely exploited his imperial subjects because … power rested on suppression of opposition, an enlarged police force and direct control either by France or by rulers imposed by France.

Developing an argument

Though clear, this is a very 'one-way' argument and ignores possible benefits for the conquered territories. It is as if the question had read 'Show how…'

Page 79

Eliminate irrelevance

Napoleon looked carefully at the divisions between the allies' powers at the Congress of Vienna and this encouraged him to risk another adventure. ~~He arrived at the south of France and then moved northwards where he gained more and more support. A force sent against him did not follow orders to oppose him. He stepped forward and opened his coat, daring them to fire.~~ The rapid flight of Louis XVIII and the limited resistance showed that the restored monarchy had a limited impact on the people. ~~This was not the first daring adventure that Napoleon had undertaken in his career and he still believed that the same destiny that had seemed to guide him in Italy in 1796 or in his bid to take power in 1799 or in the daring campaign of 1805 would lead to success.~~ However, the new constitution was not much of an advance on the Charter given by Louis XVIII and, though Napoleon raised an army, too much was dependent on military success. Given the limited successes of his last campaigns, there was not much hope that he would remain in power simply by fighting some brilliant battles. Support drained away quickly and everything turned on the campaign in Belgium. But even if that had been successful, there was no certainty that the allies would accept Napoleon.

Page 81

Develop the detail

The answer could include details of the Sixth Coalition and why it was more powerful and determined. The issue of the failure to negotiate could be developed, as this is a key element. The failure to maintain support could be expanded.

Spectrum of importance

Many might look at 3 as leading to some of the other factors but there is no set answer.